A JOURNAL OF CONTEMPORARY WRITING

IRISH PAGES

DUILLÍ ÉIREANN

IRISH PAGES is a biannual journal (Spring-Summer, Autumn-Winter), edited in Belfast and publishing, in equal measure, writing from Ireland and overseas. It appears at the end of each six-month period.

Its policy is to publish poetry, short fiction, essays, creative non-fiction, memoir, essay reviews, nature-writing, translated work, literary journalism, and other autobiographical, historical, religious and scientific writing of literary distinction. There are no standard reviews or narrowly academic articles. Irish-language and Scots writing are published in the original, with English translations or glosses. IRISH PAGES is a non-partisan, non-sectarian, culturally ecumenical, and wholly independent journal. It endorses no political outlook or cultural tradition, and has no editorial position on the constitutional question. Its title refers to the island of Ireland in a purely apolitical and geographic sense, in the same manner of The Church of Ireland or the Irish Sea.

The sole criteria for inclusion in the journal are the distinction of the writing and the integrity of the individual voice. Equal editorial attention will be given to established, emergent and new writers.

The views expressed in IRISH PAGES are not necessarily those of the Editors. The journal is published by Irish Pages Ltd, a non-profit organization.

Submissions are welcome but must be accompanied by return postage or an international reply coupon. No self-addressed envelope is required. Reporting time is nine months. If work is accepted, a copy on disk may be requested.

Your subscription is essential to the independence and survival of the journal. Subscription rates are £16stg/€26/$45 for one year. Visit our website at www.irishpages.org for a subscription form or to order online. Credit cards are welcome.

IRISH PAGES
129 Ormeau Road
Belfast BT7 1SH

Advisory Board
Jonathan Allison
William Crawley
John Gray
Maureen Mackin
Bernard O'Donoghue
Daniel Tobin

Legal Advice: Kathy Mathews, Johnsons Law,
Belfast/Dublin/London

*IRISH PAGES is designed by Alicia McAuley Publishing Services
and set in 12/14.5 Monotype Perpetua. It is printed in Belfast
by Nicholson & Bass.*

*This issue has been generously asssisted by Foras na Gaeilge
and the Arts Councils of Northern and Southern Ireland.*

ISBN 978-0-9561046-0-1

Supported by
The National Lottery®
through the Arts Council of Northern Ireland

Foras na Gaeilge

Ulster-Scots Agency
Boord o Ulstèr-Scotch

IRISH PAGES

CHRIS AGEE, *Editor*

CATHAL Ó SEARCAIGH, *Irish Language Editor*

ANDREW PHILIP (Scotland) *and* STEPHEN DORNAN (Ulster),
Scots Language Editors

SEÁN MAC AINDREASA, *Managing Editor*

ELIZABETH SWITAJ, *Assistant Managing Editor*

ANDREW EATON, *Editorial Assistant*
AONGHAS MACLEÒID, *Editorial Assistant*
KATE MIDDLETON, *Editorial Assistant*

EDITED IN BELFAST
VOLUME 7, NUMBER 2

IRISH PAGES
DUILLÍ ÉIREANN

VOLUME 7, NUMBER 2

CONTENTS

Memory

Titanic *Graving Dock, Harland & Wolff, Belfast, 2010*
By Bobbie Hanvey

AFTERMATH

Kerry Hardie

On the plane of between ... after the death of a brother.

Two summers ago we spent a couple of weeks in a cottage on the Iveragh Peninsula in County Kerry. For the first week the rain was relentless. Out on the side of a mountain with two young spaniels who needed exercise, I lost my footing in driving rain and fell into a bog hole. Flailing around in the half light in water up to my chest, I made contact with something bubbling and putrid and mostly submerged. I was sharing the bog hole with the rotting remnants of a long-dead sheep.

Unlike the sheep, I managed to crawl from the hole, then stumbled back down the mountain into a steaming hot bath. My clothes went into the washing machine, came out, went in. Again and again and again. There'd been a scummy slick on the bog water, a skim of greyish bubbles and strands of old wool. It must have been the oils from the animal's body. Now I couldn't get the death-smell out of my clothes, no matter how often I washed them. Nor out of my skin though I scrubbed it with sweet-smelling soap.

I became obsessively conscious of it. I would sit at my table in the rented house, unable to work. There were spreading brown stains on the plastered wall beside me that came from the heat of the huge old chimney-flue behind the wall. I imagined the warmth of the room was increasing the smell and drawing it from my skin. I moved downstairs but it was no better.

A few days later we went to a friend's for dinner, a house on the edge of the sea. I sat in a room full of books and talk and food, a life far removed from the bog and moor and silence of the mountains. Self-conscious, I put my arm behind my back, but an arm is attached to the body and can't be altogether dispensed with. The smell came slinking out into the room and licked itself round me. Convinced that it was rank and authentic, I began to explain to the woman I was talking to. She said she had a wonderful nose and demanded a sniff at my arm. I held it out.

"Imagination", she pronounced decisively.

I thought at the time that it must have been a neurotic reaction. I have since been surprised at the number of people who confirmed the experience and spoke of a similar obsession with smell following contact with something dead.

Perhaps, like death itself, the smell stays in the nostrils long after the actual occasion has passed. Perhaps the body holds onto the smell of another body's demise, even if the body isn't human. Worse if it is human: war diaries all record being overwhelmed by smell. Presumably it's the shock of premonition: the recognition by the body of its own mortality, its terror at the unavoidable abandonment that is coming to it.

———

A young woman whose father was killed in a car crash told me of her inability to manage her life for a long time after the event. As well as the grief that overwhelmed her in the immediate aftermath, she described its unpredictable reappearance in the most unlikely times and situations. She also spoke of making stupid mistakes, of confusion in managing the simplest transactions, of losing words in company.

She said that 50 years ago in Ireland she'd have slipped a black arm-band onto her sleeve every morning for a year before she left the house. She talked of how, in modern Celtic-Tiger Ireland, she had longed for an arm-band because it would have explained her situation. It would have been like the red light flashing on the car that drives ahead of a vehicle that's too long or too wide or too slow for the road that it's travelling.

Look out. Here comes grief.

Everyone stops or pulls in to the side and makes allowances.

That's completely gone now. We still do the death-thing – the wake, the vigil, the removal and the funeral. It's very communal, very intense. But when all that's done we get up in the morning thinking that somehow it's over. We expect ourselves to be able to act as though this event that blocked out the stars has safely moved into the past. We are unprepared for the sheer intensity of the pain that's about to kick in.

But the death-smell is in our nostrils and in our clothes and deep in the pores of our skin. Though strangers cannot smell it, we can smell nothing else.

———

When death happens we find that a part of us already knows quite a lot about the corporeal side of what has to be coped with. We may not have fought in a war or worked in an abattoir or fallen into a bog-hole with a dead sheep, but we've all experienced the private reality of our own physicality, we know about blood and pain and shit and our own fear of it. We are generally less overwhelmed by the sight of death than we think we will be.

What is so surprising is that we have supposed that seeing the corpse is the greater part of what we will have to deal with.

The suffering that we experience at the death of someone we love very much – especially when that death is untimely and we feel that a life has not been lived – is unimaginably painful. What is even more shocking is that there is nothing that can be done to relieve this pain, we just have to trudge through each day and endure it. Sometimes we think we can't.

Everyone tells us this pain will lessen but they speak from a reality that has very little to do with us, even if they have themselves experienced what we are now going through. So it isn't that we don't believe them: we simply stare at them blankly, waiting for their mouths to stop moving.

That they are speaking from a different reality is literally true. Death pushes us deeper into our lives, we act and react from a place that is not normally accessible to us, we experience phenomena that at other times we would be unable to experience. Where does the spirit go when it leaves the body behind it? I don't know, but I think there is an intermediate stage when it still has occasional access to the life it previously occupied, however briefly.

So immediately following an important death there is the possibility of an interchange that would not otherwise happen and that mostly disappears once we have moved back into our normal lives and the dead have moved on to other realms. This can be both comforting and disturbing. With the passing of time it happens less frequently and is less intense. Both parties are moving away from each other and are becoming established in their changed state of being. Slowly the suffering of the person who loves lessens until the day comes when there are moments when it is almost absent. If these moments join up for even a brief period of time, then we are capable of relaxing into a state of non-suffering. Once non-suffering becomes established there is again the possibility of joy. (Strangely it is possible to experience joy when in a state of physical suffering, but emotional suffering cancels it out.)

The return of joy, however fleeting, is usually accompanied by feelings of betrayal and hence the return of suffering. A yo-yo movement has begun.

There is a gap in the intensity of our grief so life rushes in. Fear of the return of intense suffering is almost as painful as the suffering itself.

People talk a lot about anger following a death, but perhaps this anger is simply a variation on suffering — a kind of substitute that happens when the truly devastating pain has eased a little and it is possible to be angry at the person who has died for causing it. If the relationship was complicated and there were a lot of unresolved issues then the feeling of abandonment that has caused the anger is more intense. There are also the bubbles of gas that rise up from the body in the bog-hole. Sometimes we discover things we did not know, are brought face to face with aspects of the dead person they have concealed from us. It doesn't have to be the mistress who turns up at the funeral. There are often small ambushes, many of them simply things we chose not to see.

The emotional instability around anger, betrayal and pain bring us close to chaos. But a return to "normality" would mean an odd kind of loss. Somewhere there is an awareness in us that we are living on a different plane, and somewhere we also crave the purity and intensity of this plane — as those whose lungs are used to high clean air crave relief from the smog and fumes of a city. On this other level it is possible to be alone with your dead and to feel their presence. This is hard to let go of, though it must be accomplished. It is the only thing that will bring about the release of the dead. To dwell there too long is not our purpose in life. Somehow we must find the grace to accept the living.

I think we are "saved" back into life by matter. The weeks and months pass and the flesh we inhabit reasserts its dominance. The weight returns to the things of the world and the strange clear light that we lived in becomes too strange and clear. The disturbing feelings of guilt at the prospect of a return to a state of being that is closer to normality begin to recede. We want food, warmth, density. The mountain in the driving rain. The wet dogs drying in the heat of a fire that is contained and domesticated, its ferocious energy channelled through a hearth and a chimney.

———

But we have experienced that energy, and the plaster on our wall is discoloured and disfigured like the flue-wall in that cottage in the mountains. We know its power. Every time the phone rings our equanimity is shattered — we are back in the bog-hole, floundering around in disaster.

And the reality of our existing disaster makes the potential for further disaster unlimited. We have lost all trust in dailiness. No amount of reassurance can counter the ongoing psychic disturbance our dreams convey to us. All is not right. It will never be right in quite the same way again. We have made contact with what is deep inside us and also with what is beyond us. There is a pathway opened between them.

It is important to remember that the dead do not belong to us. When a death is that of a young child it is all but impossible to grasp this. A young child is dependent and in our care. When they die we feel that our roles continue. This is also true of adults where the parents and siblings have had a strong nurturing role. They know they must cede this role to the wife, husband or partner, in death as in life, but the weight of years makes that harder to do. There are so many photographs and memories that happened before the new union. In death, the first family yearns to reclaim its child. The partner is also staking a claim. Everything gets confused. Hence the unseemly scramble for possessions after a death.

Obtaining a possession is like proof of ownership. Possessions are valuable, not for themselves, but for their relationship to the person who has died. A lighter, a wallet, a hairbrush — intimate things that were used every day — become charged. We imagine they retain something of their owner. By treasuring them we think we can somehow prolong their belonging among us.

But the dead belong to themselves. They have completed their lives, even if the death came about through violence. Somewhere a contract has been signed off on and nothing will undo what has been done. Nor can we follow them or hold onto them once they have ceased to meet with us on the plane of between. We can only cherish what we had and let them go.

Kerry Hardie was born in Singapore in 1951 and grew up in Co Down. She is the author of six collections of poems, most recently The Ash and the Oak and the Wild Cherry Tree *(The Gallery Press, 2012) and two novels,* Hannie Bennett's Winter Marriage *and* The Bird Woman *(Harper Collins, 2000 and 2006). She is a member of Aosdána, and lives in Milltown, Co Kilkenny.*

PARABLE OF A SUMMER

Chris Agee

A cool mental dew.

Another call, email, task, list, purchase, repair, reconstruction, focus, meeting, movement. Another *thing*. Above all, in all this — covering all this — another thing-to-do. What might it mean, in an ontological sense? It is, I'd say, Roth's "dream of endlessness" — the assumption, on some primordial psychological level, owing to each past day's renewal of *presence* present, that we will never end. At some point, it all seems to say, we will reach the paradisical terminus of completion, the plenitude, or platitude, of *everything done*.

But for most of us, I daresay, looking back, it will never have happened. Paradise not lost, but unmaterialized. More of an Elysium of shadowy tasks in the foreground of missed existence. More *Microsoft Office* than the *Word* of life's real presence. Sisyphus in the half-life of his daily incline, daily decline.

Up above us, like some caul of techno-bioluminescence we've lately developed, the jellyfish of new communication floats in the ether of near space, moored to its satellites. It is clear that a large proportion of humanity, already, cannot elude it for more than a few days, or contemplate living without it.

———

Birdwatching is subtle. One of the eye's subtle arts. An art, too, of the ear. And extremely ancient: the stuff of augury and omen. It is strange to think that these creatures might be the shrunken dwarves of pterodactyls and dinosaural colour.

You can see, though, why many will see nothing in it. Its narrow visual range, its endless repetitions.

A few swallows pirouetting like jets through the morning yard — their blue-black backs, their white bellies. The secretive flash of the golden oriole. An owl taking wing out of the almonds against the last light of the valley. Flocks of little brown birds, unidentified, seeking gleanings at raked dawn on our old gravelly road between parched grasses, disturbed into flight by an opened door. The strange grace of the house bats tumbling headlong through the same yard as soon as dark falls. Up from Africa in April, the hoarse serenade of nightingales, trilling and squeaking in the crisp and starry night. Could there really be much in it?

But it teaches you to attend. To wait on the small thing and the little surprise. To abandon the pseudo-cosmic disease for the narrower reaches of a microcosmos. To plumb intently, as with augury or Newton, just one moment's becoming on the ground of physical being. Where that small surprise can take wing into the imaginations of one's full attention.

And on almost every occasion of such attention, there *are* surprises. Like one time when a small bird with rufous back, buff belly and black mask alighted in sunshine on the almond sapling in front of the terrace. The species is common, if still unidentified; but I had never quite noticed the marvel of its glossy back, its rufous sheen.

Till that minute on the morning in question. I might not have stepped one leg up on the wall of the terrace and looked in that direction. I might have been thinking of emails.

Updike has spoken of the increasing "dephysicalization" of contemporary culture. Is this, then, now the one globalized, dominant ontology-ideology? If so, in this sense, for me in any event, a rufous gloss must always trump – or out-Trump – any email.

———

People in the village are always giving each other little gifts. It is a kind of barter of goodwill and neighbourly feeling.

One morning I saw an old neighbour's wife meet Jasinka, a younger neighbour, on the crumbling tarmac that runs by our house through weathered stone walls. The Žrnovo church clock was just striking its nine chimes. After the loud and public greetings that are typical, she immediately gave Jasinka a plastic bag of tomatoes from her garden. Whether the tomatoes were intended for Jasinka, or whether they were to be unloaded on the first friend or neighbour she encountered on the road, was unclear. It always is …

Another morning, our neighbour Petar, who seldom visits, suddenly appeared round the corner of the house from the tarmac lane. The terrace was still in shade and I was taking an early breakfast alone. He was shirtless and in sandals, with a straw hat like Huck Finn's. He brought me a bag of two cucumbers and four tomatoes, of the heartshaped local variety, always very good. Perhaps it was also an occasion to remark on my three haystacks: that after my last misjudgement with petrol in May, scorching the cypress, they should not be burnt until October. The island's summer tinderbox of scrub forest, parched vegetation and grassy olive groves was a perennial threat.

His gift lifted my spirits at the start of another hot day. It was like a cool mental dew in the optimism of the morning. Its common quality, over time, across village space, partly informs, and partly inspired, this prose.

———

A black ant scampers across the creamy white of a limestone jamb.

Dalmatian light and dark.

Everything — *every thing* — is interesting.

Later, not far from the stone threshold, another ant — or, maybe, the same one — hauls its awn of straw, with Sisyphean purpose, towards the Eocene's version of our own technohive.

Žrnovo, Croatia, 2009

Chris Agee is the Editor of this journal. His third collection of poems, Next to Nothing *(Salt, 2009), was shortlisted for the 2010 Ted Hughes Award for New Work in Poetry, funded by the Poet Laureate and organized by the Poetry Society in London. He is currently working on a fourth collection.*

from MEMOIRS

Tom Mac Intyre

Bends and brows.

MICKY DEASY'S ACCOUNT OF ROETHKE ON INISHBOFIN

A momentum.

We were diggin' a grave that mornin', ould Hannah Scofield for burial, delicate woman all her life, and yet verra healthy. Verra healthy. Roethke – I remember it as well as bread – appeared on the road above the graveyard, sippin' whiskey from a roomy bottle. He studied us, said nothing, moved on, without so much as a wave moved on. We knew he'd be back. And he was. Took him about an hour. Less. This time the bottle was filled with sand. He gave us a look, and, top of his voice, he shouts – "Fine day to be diggin' a grave! Fine day to be diggin' a grave!" And lets fly with the bottle. It brushed the hair on my head, broke into smithereens against a handy tombstone. Someone prayin' for me. "Fine day to be diggin' a grave!" They took him away that evenin'. Quiet as a pet mouse. The Big House in Ballinasloe. Found his way back to The States. Poet. Comical class of a man. Only yesterday I was thinkin' of him. Yesterday mornin'. I'm on the pier, mailboat ready to haul anchor. And what do I see? A sack filled with winkles, export for some Paris eatin'-house. Peter Halloran beside it, he made a few bob at that game. Only wait. Written on the sack – "Saginaw Bean Company, Saginaw, Michigan". Roethke, begod. He used them sacks to lug his books, wherever he'd be goin'. I wanted that sack – as a momentum, like – but I couldn't interfere. Laid a hand on it, maybe. Aye. Back to The States with him, after the week in Ballinasloe. Died soon after, I heard. I liked Roethke. Soft something to him. And something never tamed. Market Gardenin', they were in, the family. Comical class of a man. "Fine day to be diggin' a grave!" There y'are now. There y'are.

THE FORT

Written.

It wasn't that far from the grandmother's farmhouse, yet it seemed and was in a world of its own. Fort meant "fairy-fort", invoked will-o'-the-wisp, stray sod, phantom of a storied grey horse dead, long dead. A plague of white mice had taken over the fort a few years back, I was told. Winter visit. Hibernation! Came. And went with the spring. Just like that. It looked like any other field – but only if you had sleep in your eyes. The gate into it was at a bend of the lane, darkened by a few chestnut trees. I'd been told not to go near it. But at six years of age I knew no fear. Dread? I knew what dread was – shadow on the wall, nothing on the floor, and it was a fine sense of dread was pulling me towards a meeting with the fort field. Must meeting. My step a pilgrim step. So be it.

Came the morning. Ten o'clock, and all's well. Fine day for a hunt! The uncle was off to the town on his bike – he went for the paper every day, rain or shine. Jemmy Swan, the hired "boy", was clearing a shuck at a safe remove from my planned excursion. The grandmother was pounding praties in the kitchen. I slipped out the door and floated to the first bend of the lane. Perhaps I walked then for a bit – there was no hurry on me, after all. I'd left hurry behind, I was already on some other plane of existence. What plane? I could never have defined it – but that it had eased me into a condition of the weightless is certain. I was wearing a red gansy, I noticed. Good. Purple, maybe, better – but, instinct told me, red pertained. A humming silence. Spirals of bird-song. Mackerel sky. Mares' tails. What was that a sign of? Bounty: when you're doing what you should be doing at six-and-a-half, everything is bounty. Everything a sign.

Shadowland of the chestnut trees. The gate to the fort field. I shinned the rusty bars. I was in the fort field. Steep rise of it before me. The fairy-fort. I'd heard that in one such near Kells – only up the road – they'd found a mini-sized waistcoat, rich material, beautifully fashioned. Someone took it to a master-tailor in Dublin, and, withholding any detail as to its origin, asked for a comment. "That garment", came the verdict, "was made by no human hand". I studied the slope, the ground whispery quiet underfoot. A church bell tolled from Cross Chapel a mile away. Somebody's burial. "Beryl", the grandmother would say. She'd wonder where I'd gone. Would she pursue? She might – but I'd no fret. She wasn't to know where I was on the thirty acres that were in it – every acre alive with some lure or other but none, it had to be admitted, to match the fort field. Still. I felt safe. And happily imperilled. Half-way up the slope. I'm studying a plump thistle. My own height. The fat of it. Raised my head. Now d'ye mind? I had company. There was a white calf in the fort field. Look. Right there. On the brow of the hill. Shining white. A lamp. A summons. Breathing summons. An antic pulse travelled me, head to toe. Call it what it was. A shiver.

Maybe it was the summer day was in it. Maybe it was something else – the light, my eyes that morning, was I *seeing* better? Whatever it was, certain it was, never had whiter calf walked the earth. A sumptuous creature. Looking at me. Not looking at me. But, rest assured, aware of my approach. Not in the least disturbed by my intrusion. Was I expected? Why not? Ordinary rules didn't apply – how could they? – in the confines of the fairy-fort. White of the calf more white as the seconds flew. White of creation! Calf a few weeks old. Steady on the pins. Watching me, sidelong gaze, *relishing*, I'd go so far as, my arrival. I could have said "Hello", but knew enough to keep my gob shut. Maybe I should have bowed. If I failed in that, certain it is that I deferred. Already I knew I was stepping into my life. Wisdom of this calf's eyes. Presence.

All right. Calm. Some version of calm. I'm halted a few feet away from the whitest calf ever was. And we're examining other, rather, it came to me, as if this meeting had been arranged in the long ago, in the now, in the yet to be. We had an expression at school – "I was poxed." *Poxed* meant lucky beyond all notions of lucky. I remember thinking to myself – the minute I spot my white beauty on the slope above me – thinking that, for whatever reason, every good fortune was meant to be mine, from this out, on foot of a meeting, unimaginable surprise, and entirely forecastable, with a white calf, shriven, shapely, expectant – *there*, there was the crucial flavour – the white calf was waiting for me, this meeting was – what? "Written", as my father might say. A favourite word of his. It's *written*. That was *written*. Meant to be. Unavoidable. A compass. A road.

Everything now happening at tremendous speed. And, also, as if we had all time in the world. I hadn't touched the calf yet. That must happen, had to, it was in the air. *Written*. We were now looking at each other like old friends – have I said that before? Those large valleyed eyes. A gentleness you'd fear to ponder, so delicate its sway. It seemed we'd been there, conversing, with years. Suddenly – and yet leisurely – I knew what my next move must be. I simply grabbed the calf by the tail. I tugged. The calf took off – and we're flying through the air. My story-telling career, my born life, had commenced, and, in the bosom of morning, I'm singin' – "*Sally, tell the mother I'll never come back!*"

———

JUST LIKE THAT

Mind yourself.

It happened so simply. Across the dance-floor she gave me what we called "the sheep's eyes". "Did she give you the sheep's eyes?" "Yes." And you gave her the invisible nod? Yes. So we danced. Introductions. Her name was Given, Anna, peeler's daughter. She was fair or she was dark, merry or solemn – it didn't matter. She was willing. Needful. Even. I had been chosen. She'd be eighteen, say, of an age with me. The band played on. Was she a virgin? I didn't think so. But she'd found herself one. *Gaudeamus igitur*, sang my trembling flesh. The dance-hall was packed – yet it seemed roomy. She was roomy. Was I? In no time, little talk, we were leaving the band, the dancers, to it. Why delay?

A driven summer night. We were on a lake-shore. Timbered shore. We were under a tree. A fir-tree, Dionysus tree. Lights of the hall, the distant band, watching over us. Vaguely. Neutrally. "Would ye back a gate?" – sang the moment. Would ye back a tree? Fading foxtrot. Cool of the night. Our clothing – waist down – seemed to melt. And I was inside her. Warm she was. I came quickly, without reserve, my blithe assumption being that she'd chosen a safe time. We didn't go back to the dance-hall. I walked her to her home, nearby. We kissed. Parted. Rating for the event? Bit of a let-down. But. Something out of the way? You could say that.

Next morning, up on ten o'clock, I was in the arms of a Carmelite priest in a mid-Dublin church, confessing my sin, abject, stained, disordered. In flitters. I moaned contrition, submitted to castigation, staggered on to the street, stumbled home. Spoke to no one of the adventure. I was queasily aware that something of moment had happened. My tastebuds had been soused. Uncertainly, confusedly. Anna Given. Unlikely turquoise eyes. "Mind yourself", she said as we parted. She hesitated, smiled, added – "You know the one about the mother saying goodbye to Setanta, an' him heading for Emhain Macha, did they tell you that at any school or other?" I shook my head. "Tell me, Anna." She kissed me, motherly kiss – and more in the tastebuds, much more. "She said to him – 'Emhain Macha. A hard road that, son – and The Forest before you.'"

We shared our best kiss; never saw her from that day to this. An omission. Certainly that. Sins of omission. They're the ones, I'm told, they're the ones howl for forgiveness.

———

FIRE

Live with it.

It was dusk. Sunday evening. Forgotten how the word came – "The Hotel's on fire." And people gathered. Coming from Middle Quarter, our direction, a road above and back from the action offered an inviting platform. A road, a wall to lean on, the clear view. Half of us settled there, half dozen, say. The rest, only the slightest hesitation, strode on down to join those already engaged in fighting the flames.

Well. You'd pause to catch breath, and then – forget it. Too much happening. It wasn't a raging fire – yet – but you could see the flames, *measure* them, spot the human chain passing buckets of water, sea-water, to douse, if possible, the outbreak. We hadn't quite settled, it's only fair to say; the invitation – go on down, join the resistance – was still there, several times I was on my way, but a point came, and we thought of participation, that kind of participation, no more. We were content to watch. The numbers on the job below seemed sufficient. Too many cooks, and so on. We snuggled to the wall. Gripped. Fire grips, guarantee you that, friend. Prometheus, yer man, has a lot to answer for.

Time seems to alter in such circumstances – don't know why. The conjurer magic of theatre? Because the viewer, disengaged, is so engaged? Strange vacuum. How were they doing down there? Winning or losing – it was impossible to say. There was shadow, there was flame, splashes of light, there was noise, low noise, there was the human chain – what is it about a human chain? A brave dominant, without question. No water supply points handy or, at any rate, none of sufficient force to meet the needs of the hour. So the men, the buckets, relentlessly going to it, visible, half-visible, battle joined, flicker and purr of the avid flames, and us watching. Silent. The nest of us, held wordless, for once.

What else? An eerie flavour: we could feel the warmth of the fire. Riddle me that. Magic-lantern show? Next, no signal, it was pitch dark, and, paradoxically, everything more visible. Flash-lamps, lanterns, light from the hotel windows, car-lights. Was the valiant resistance winning or losing? Impossible to say. Everything too iffy. *Iffy*, down there, was the name of the game. Hypnotic spectacle, I have to say, what you could see of it. And the noise — that wasn't noise, really. The noise was imaginary, as far as we were concerned. Wind, likely, taking it the opposite direction. No, this was a feast of the visual, murky visual, forget the auditory. No sound score. But bewitching chiaroscuro — no scarcity of that lady. I still thought of going down (it wasn't too late, by no means) to join the redoubtable human chain, but no, no, that choice, live with it, had been made a while back, and had, by now, a sealed irrevocable something guarding it. I'd opted to stay up here — on this vantage point, I'd declared myself spectator. So be it: that's the meaning of *Amen*, isn't it?

Visibility? Was it now getting thickish dark? You could say that. Bar the scene of the action below. Disconcertingly humdrum, the hard slog of it, but also, no doubt, exciting, I thought, we thought, for those engaged in the fracas. Dangerous even. You could have explosions. This was a *fire*, remember. Anything could happen. And how silent we were, the small band of us, all male, I knew them all, neighbours. Silent as never before. Fixed. And, tap on the shoulder from an invisible hand, it came to me — you could smell it, I could smell it right into the folds of my gizzard: looking at those flames — they hadn't spread, nor had they lessened — viewing those flames, brazen snap of them now and then audible, it came to me, swept me, toxic, a question: whose side are you on, mate? You and your small band of refuseniks here in the dusk above the fray? For whom are you praying? Cheering? Churning moral support? And — lollipop sweet an' sour — came the answer: on the side of the fire. I wanted — we wanted — admit it — the fire to win. Reduce the building to ashes. No loss of life, no injured parties, but — that said — I knew, those in a knot beside me knew, I could smell it. Pong of it. We wanted the fire to win.

That realization. A baptism. *We're on the side of the fire.* We the spectators. There on our ledge. Watching the battle below, smoke and shadow, tongue of flame, the insistent low din, the *ad-hoc* fire-brigade, the chain, the human chain, water, water, obstinately sticking to it, the battle, and the flames fighting for *their* good health, their curious rights, their provender, ashes, ashes, flame, combustion, ashes the great leveller and original democrat. Go For It. We couldn't cheer but we yearned to. It was the gentlest, strangest, virus. Well-nigh tender. New. And old. We'd no defence. It took us away. Silent. The knot of us. Praying. May the fire win. Leap. Spread. Raze the building. Nobody hurt, not a soul. But ashes, no respite, leave nothing but the scarred framework, the scorched stones. Thank you.

Then it was over. Human chain won. Drove back the flames to the murky unknown from which they streamed. Like a red-letter hallucinatory fuck it was *consummatum est*, on the way to the trickeries of remembrance. Human chain won. Smell of smoke. Scorch-marks. Pints, and plenty, for the fire fighters, the eternal human chain. We didn't fancy, let's be honest, going down to back-slap, join them in the bar. We couldn't. Not didn't fancy. So what did we do? Sloped away into the night. It was night now. Good. I don't say we were ashamed. Maybe we were. Shame is a slithery boyo. We were, all right, we were the bit ashamed. Tomorrow we'd be told – "Didn't want to get your locks singed, eh? Shure we understand – and now we know yiz the bit better besides." Quite. Told the story to a buddy of mine from Nashville a long time after. One Hal Holliday. He viewed me. "You looked. You watched. You sided with the fire." Pause. Lovely loitering antebellum Nashville pause. "That's why we got fire-brigades, man."

———

THE OTHER SILENCE

Ye boy ye.

I spend lots of time on the shore these days. It pulls me, gently. Not that I'm inclined to resist, no, no. With white hair, oyster-white of the eye, comes (sometimes) a scrap of knowledge. Touching? Direction. Roads. Want to know about roads? They end. On the shore. Tarred road, by-road, highway, autobahn, all end on the shore. Where other roads begin? Oh, yes.

I am on the shore. Excitement in the wanton air. I'm, no surprise, alone. Find myself increasingly alone on that margin, and, spiced conundrum, more and more in company. Today, on the sand beside me, body of a hare, emptied body, looks like. Imagine a garment thrown away, jacket that's served its turn. Perched hard by, the hare's head. Ears on full alert, eyes strobe-lit. It's — what is it? Space-capsule. Ready for anything. Take-off. Orbit!

And I'm aware of a silence that surrounds. We've met. A long time ago, I was unwell, often been unwell, one of my healthier habits. It's winter, night, and I'm alone in the living room, standing by the window. There's rime on the pane. I'm wiping — spittle-and-thumb — the rime away. Now I can see. Snow on the lawn, silhouette of the trees, evergreen mostly. All quiet. No longer. The quiet shifts to a silence that imbrues. I can hear, fugal and murmurous, the Unknown.

Which brings me to the dove-grey horse. I met Dove-Grey first on the grandmother's farm. A brown horse there too but nobody passed any remarks. Dove-Grey took the eye, never gave it back. Why so? I didn't know but blood knew. Old expert blood, special kind of juice! When, as Dove-Grey cantered past, a fir-tree whispered, "Pale horse, pale rider", my veins raced understanding. Dove-Grey was here, powerfully, but, just as powerfully, somewhere else. Dove-Grey was. Is. Will be. Scattered your wits. Captive, you daren't caress this beauty. Your hand would come out the other side. So. You watched from an acolyte remove. Others partook of the cult. Nothing was said. Just — guard your candle, its shy flame.

We're born to forget. Seems. I forgot until I was reminded, this fine day in dark of the night. It was on an island. Do you like islands? I find them floaty, ductile, schooling. Midnight, yes, I was, fortunately, taking a ramble on heights of the eastward dunes. An old man approached. I knew him, had, indeed, recently bought his currach. Here was a boatsman born, fast friend of the tides. "Listen", he said, "the brown horse is a daylight job, any *gom* could tell you that. Dove-Grey's story is other …" And my beauty was beside us. I looked, and through Dove-Grey — transparency allowed — I could see the currach moored in the cove below. Freshly tarred, her shiny black rose and dipped against green of the wave.

A "useful meeting"! But, Habit is your only deafener. Again I disremember — meeting, offered counsel, bright transparency. I am, after all, a busy man, pelf preoccupies, cunt, cock, sultry scrotum. Let's not get into *mea culpa*. Facts, please. Right. The lambent calendar, no warning, wheels to ache and pain, falling teeth, the rheum and the rheumatics. On cue, ushers — dulcet, undemanding — arrive from the shades. It's their season! Don't ask them for identification, you know — all you need to know. It is they who introduce you — for, odds on, the last time — to an old friend, Dove-Grey. In feisty fettle. Hasn't changed since the first sighting. While back. Hello.

Dove-Grey is bridled, saddled, game for the road. Thinking, "Strange how patterned the briary world can be", I climb aboard. No creak, *nota bene*, of joint, that infirmity dissolved. And we're off. Release. Morning. Journey. I feel light, could be feather-grass, pensive shadow of feather-grass. And I hear a silence I know. Dove-Grey's hooves are soundless. Likewise bit, bridle, saddle, stirrups. No sounds now except sound of this mother silence, inviolate, beckoning …

Finally. A word on daffodils, breath of daffodils. When, regal, she came with the bouquet (this was only last week), I was in bed. Alone. Waiting for her? Could be. I should never forget this meeting. Green of the stalks, gold of the blossoms. Her reach of gentleness. Was I up to the moment? Not at all. Being on the horizontal as recipient wasn't a help. But I've no excuse, really, I've never been prepared for anything. Birth. Coupling. Separations. Next time round I may do better. Is there a next time? I don't know. Talk of it now and again.

Tell you about her? That she was a Queen, I knew, you know a Queen when you meet one. Such *puissance*. Style. Chic – I'd go so far as. She delivers the daffodils, and she's gone. I'm musing (it was December, as I write still is) – "Daffodils – harbingers of Spring – come before the swallows" – and so on. But, as you may have noticed, I'm not content, best thing to be said for me, it's been remarked, an appetite for unease. Daffodils – I'm not easy. Have they a *sotto voce* tocsin? Look it up. The father comes into this, his presbyter thumb working the pages of dictionary or reference book, that's how I recall him. I find the book, flip pages – Daffodils: *Prosperina's flower, they grace the meadows of The Underworld. Word comes from the Greek "asphodelus". Etymology unknown* … Shook, I put the book aside. Now, ye boy ye. So it was She. Dear Goddess down below. Take pause, son. Listen for a silence. That silence. And it arrives, brimming embrace. Comes a moment you begin to long for it. Court it. Head bowed, name it home.

A poet, dramatist and fiction writer in both English and Irish, Tom Mac Intyre was born in Cavan in 1931. He is the author of eight collections of poetry, most recently ABC *(2006),* Encountering Zoe *(2010), and* Poppy's Leavetaking *(2012), all from New Island. His plays for The Abbey Theatre include* The Great Hunger *(1983),* Good Evening, Mr Collins *(1997) and his version of Brian Merriman's* Cúirt An Mhean Oíche / The Midnight Court *(1999). A collection of short fiction,* The Word for Yes: New and Selected Stories, *was published by the Gallery Press in 1991. He is a member of Aosdána, and lives in Lurganboy, Co Cavan.*

SLIVER OF SKY

Barry Lopez

Confronting the trauma of sexual abuse.

One day in the fall of 1938, a man named Harry Shier entered the operating room of a Toronto hospital and began an appendectomy procedure on a prepubescent boy. He was not a trained surgeon; he nearly botched the operation, and the boy's parents reacted angrily. Suspicions about Shier's medical credentials had already surfaced among operating-room nurses, and the hospital, aware of other complaints related to Shier's groin-area operations on young boys, opened a formal investigation. By the time the hospital board determined that both his medical degree, from a European university, and his European letters of reference were fraudulent, Harry Shier had departed for the United States.

A few years later, a police officer in Denver caught Shier raping a boy in the front seat of his automobile. Shier spent a year in prison and then slipped out of Colorado. In the late 1940s, he surfaced in North Hollywood, California, as the director of a sanitarium where he supervised the treatment of people with addictions, primarily alcoholics. In the summer of 1952, at the age of seven, I was introduced to him when I visited the sanitarium with my mother.

At the time, I lived with her and my younger brother in nearby Reseda, a town in the San Fernando Valley. My parents had recently divorced, and my father had moved across the country to Florida. To support the three of us, my mother had taken a day job teaching Home Economics at a junior high school in the city of San Fernando and also a job teaching dressmaking two evenings a week at Pierce Junior College in Woodland Hills, on the far western edge of the Valley.

Early that summer, my mother had somewhat reluctantly agreed to take in a houseguest, her first cousin Evelyn Carrothers. Evelyn, who was my mother's age, lived an hour away in Long Beach and was struggling with a drinking problem. Her marriage was also in trouble. Mother couldn't accommodate Evelyn for long in our one-bedroom house, so she began inquiring among her friends about other arrangements. People advised her to call Alcoholics Anonymous. Someone in the organization's Los Angeles office suggested that she contact the North Hollywood Lodge and Sanitarium.

One morning, Mother drove us all to the facility at 12003 Riverside Drive, known then around the Valley, I would later learn, as "Shier's dryer". In those years, Shier was renowned as someone who could "cure" alcoholism. He was also able to relate sympathetically to the families of alcoholics. When we arrived at the clinic, Mother introduced my four-year-old brother and me to "Dr" Shier. We shook hands with him, and he escorted the two of us to the sanitarium's kitchen, where we each selected a fresh doughnut from an array laid out on trays for the patients – frosted, sugared, glazed, covered with sprinkles. A nice man. I remember the building's corridors reeked that morning of something other than disinfectant. Paraldehyde, I was later informed, which Shier used liberally to sedate his patients.

Shortly after Evelyn had, in Shier's estimation, recovered enough to return to Long Beach – she would begin drinking again and, a year later, would return to his facility – he started dropping by our home in Reseda. He had gotten to know something of Mother's marital and financial situation from Evelyn, and during one of his early visits he told Mother that he was concerned: her income was not, in his view, commensurate with her capabilities. He said he might be able to do something about that. (Mother's divorce settlement required my father to send her ten dollars a month in child support – an obligation he rarely met, according to correspondence I would later find.) Shier said that one of his former patients was in a position to speak with the school board about Mother's value to the school system. This appeal was apparently made, and a short while later she received a small increase in salary.

She was grateful. Harry was pleased to help. Shier conducted himself around Mother like someone considering serious courtship. She was a handsome woman of 39, he a short, abrasively self-confident, balding man of 56. He complimented her on the way she was single-handedly raising her two polite, neatly dressed sons. He complimented her on her figure. Occasionally he'd take her hand or caress her lightly on the shoulder. After a while, Shier began dropping by the house in the evening, just as my brother and I were getting into our pajamas. He'd bring a tub of ice cream along, and the four of us would have dessert together. One evening he arrived without the ice cream. He'd forgotten. He suggested I accompany him to the grocery store, where I could pick out a different dessert for each of us.

A few minutes after we left the house, he pulled his car up alongside a tall hedge on an unlit residential street off Lindley Avenue. He turned me to the side, put me face-down on the seat, pulled down my pajama bottoms, and pushed his erect penis into my anus. As he built toward his climax he told me, calmly but emphatically, that he was a doctor, that I needed treatment, and that we were not going to be adding to Mother's worries by telling her about my problem.

Shier followed this pattern of sexual assault with me for almost four years. He came by the house several times a month and continued to successfully direct Mother's attention away from what he was doing. It is hard to imagine, now, that no one suspected what was going on. It is equally difficult, even for therapists, to explain how this type of sexual violence can be perpetuated between two human beings for years without the victim successfully objecting. Why, people wonder, does the evidence for a child's resistance in these circumstances usually seem so meager? I believe it's because the child is too innocent to plan effectively, and because, from the very start, the child faces a labyrinth of confused allegiances. I asked myself questions I couldn't answer: Do I actually need protection in this situation? From what, precisely? I was bewildered by what was happening. How could I explain to my mother what I was doing? Physical resistance, of course, is virtually impossible for most children. The child's alternatives, as I understand them, never get much beyond endurance and avoidance – and speculation about how to encourage intervention.

An additional source of confusion for me was the belief that I had been chosen as a special patient by Harry Shier, an esteemed doctor and the director of a prestigious institution. A weird sense of privilege was attached to Shier's interest in me, and to the existence of an unspecified medical condition too serious or exotic to share with Mother. Also, being the elder son in a lower-middle-class and fatherless family, I came to feel – or he encouraged me to feel – that I was shouldering an important responsibility for my family. I understood that I was helping my family, and he complimented me on my maturity.

When Shier came to our house he would inform Mother that we were just going out to get some ice cream together, or, on a Saturday afternoon, that he was going to take me to an early movie, and then maybe out to dinner at the Sportsmen's Lodge on Ventura Boulevard in Studio City. We would say goodbye and he would walk me to his car and we would drive off. If it was dark, he'd pull over soon in a secluded spot and rape me in the front seat; or we'd go to the movie and he'd force my head into his lap for a while, pushing at me through his trousers; or it would be dinner at the restaurant, where we'd hook our trout in a small pool for the chef to cook, and then he'd drive on to the sanitarium, where he'd park behind the single-story building. He'd direct me up an outside staircase to a series of rotting duckboards that led across the clinic's flat roof to a locked door, the outside entrance to a rooftop apartment, where I was to wait. He'd enter the front of the building, check on his patients, say good night to the nurses, and ascend an inside staircase to reach the interior door of his studio-size quarters. I'd see the lights go on inside. A moment later he'd open the door to the roof and pull me in.

One night in these chambers, after he was through with me, he took a medical text from a bookshelf. He sat me down beside him on the edge of the bed and showed me black-and-white photographs of men's genitals ravaged by syphilis. This, he said, was what came from physical intimacy with women.

In bed with him, I would try to maneuver myself so I could focus on the horizontal sliver of sky visible between the lower edge of the drawn blinds and the white sill of the partially open window. Passing clouds, a bird, the stars.

From time to time, often on the drive back to my home, Shier would remind me that if I were ever to tell anyone, if the treatments were to stop, he would have no choice but to have me committed to an institution. And then, if I were no longer around for my family ... I'd seen how he occasionally slipped Mother a few folded bills in my presence. It would be best, I thought, if I just continued to be the brave boy he said I was.

I know the questions I initially asked myself afterward about these events were not very sophisticated. For example: Why hadn't Shier also molested my younger brother? My brother, I conjectured, had been too young in 1952, only four years old; later, with one brother firmly in hand, Shier had probably considered pursuing the other too much of a risk. (When we were older, my brother told me that Shier had molested him, several times, in the mid-1950s. I went numb with grief. After the four years of sexual violence with Shier were over, what sense of self-worth I still retained rested mainly with a conviction that, however I might have debased myself with Shier, I had at least protected my brother — and also probably saved my family from significant financial hardship. Further shame would come after I discovered that our family had never been in serious financial danger, that Mother's earnings had covered our every necessity, and more.)

My mother remarried in 1956. We moved to New York City, where my stepfather lived, and I never again saw the malachite-green-and-cream-colored Pontiac Chieftain pulling up in front of our house on Calvert Street. After we moved into my stepfather's apartment, I felt a great sense of freedom. I was so very far away now from Harry Shier. A new school, a new neighborhood, new friends. I had surfaced in another ocean. This discovery of fresh opportunity, however, which sometimes gave way to palpable euphoria, I nevertheless experienced as unreliable. I couldn't keep a hold on it. And then, two years after we moved east, when I was thirteen, Harry Shier flew into New York and my sense of safety collapsed. He arrived with my stepfather at our vacation home on the Jersey Shore one summer evening in 1958. He was my parents' guest for the weekend. A surprise for the boys.

Weren't we pleased?

The next morning, a Saturday, while my parents were preparing breakfast in the kitchen, Shier eased open the door of my attic bedroom and closed it quietly behind him. He walked wordlessly to the edge of my bed, his lips twitching in a characteristic pucker, his eyes fixed on mine. When he reached under the sheet I kicked at him and sprang from the bed, grabbing a baseball bat that was leaning against the headboard. Naked, cursing, swinging at him with the bat, I drove him from the room and slammed the door.

While I dressed, he began a conversation downstairs with my parents.

Eavesdropping on them from the hallway next to the kitchen door, I heard Shier explain that I needed to be committed. He described – in grave tones, which gave his voice a kind of Delphic weight – how I was prone to delusions, a dangerous, potentially violent boy. Trouble ahead. Through the hinge gap in the doorway, I studied my mother and stepfather seated with him at the breakfast table. Their hands were folded squarely on the oilcloth. They took in Shier's measured, professional characterization with consternation and grief. In that moment, I couldn't bring myself to describe for them what he had done. The thought of the change it would bring to our lives was overwhelming; and, regardless, my own situation felt far too precarious. Having abruptly gained the security of a family with a devoted father, I could now abruptly lose it.

I left the house without delay, to play pickup baseball with my friends. In the afternoon I rode off alone on my bicycle to the next town inland. When I returned that evening, I learned that Shier had asked my stepfather to drive him straight back to New York that morning so that he could catch a plane west from Idlewild. I had insulted the doctor, my mother told me, and embarrassed the family. She presented his analysis of my behavior. When I tried to object, her response was, "But he's a doctor!"

Shier, she said, would confer with her and my stepfather in a few days by telephone, about accommodations for me in Los Angeles.

I was not, finally, sent to California, though the reason for this was never discussed with me. If my parents harbored any misgivings about Shier, I didn't hear them. I studied hard, came home on time, did my chores: I continued to behave as a dutiful son, a boy neither parent would willingly give up.

The trauma stayed with me, however, and in the spring of 1962, when I was 17, I gave in to a state of depression. I had become confused about my sexual identity and was haunted by a sense of contamination, a feeling that I had been rendered worthless as a man because of what I had done.

When I was immobilized in the elaborate web of Shier's appetites and undone by his ploys to ensure his own safety, I had assumed I was the only boy he was involved with. It was the sudden realization that there might have been – probably were – others, and that he might still be raping boys in California, that compelled me to break my silence and risk, I believed, disastrous humiliation. I phoned my stepfather at his office. He agreed to meet me in the lobby of the New York Athletic Club on Central Park South, where I thought he would feel comfortable.

He strode impatiently into his club that afternoon and took a seat opposite me in one of the lobby's large leather chairs. He was a busy man, but he was prepared to listen. I gave him a brief account of Shier's behavior and of my history with him, and I made two requests of him. First, that he never tell anyone what had happened; if he ever came to believe that Mother had to know, he was to let me tell her. Second, that he help me stop Shier. He listened with rising interest and increasing ire. He was especially angry, I later realized, at the idea that he had been duped by Shier that summer in New Jersey.

Early the next morning, he took a plane to Los Angeles, and late that same afternoon he met with two LAPD detectives. When he returned to New York three days later, my stepfather told me that the detectives he'd spoken with were going to scrutinize everything – the North Hollywood Lodge and Sanitarium, Shier's criminal record, his network of acquaintances. They were going to gather all the evidence. I only needed to be patient. The detectives would contact us.

That week gave way to another. My stepfather waved off my anxious inquiries. He was in touch with the detectives, he said. They were working on it. When I finally confronted him, he admitted that, in consultation with the detectives, he had decided it would be too great an undertaking for me to go up against such a clever deviant, to endure cross-examination in a trial. So he was choosing not to press charges. Besides, he said, Shier had bolted as soon as he had suspected an investigation was under way.

A week or so later, my stepfather told me that he had just heard from the LAPD detectives that Harry Shier had been killed – an automobile accident in Arizona. This was, I now believe, my stepfather's preemptive effort to force closure.

In 2003, 41 years after these conversations with my stepfather and some years into my own effort to comprehend the psychological effects of what had happened to me, I phoned the LAPD. An officer there, an intermediary, was able to locate one of the two long-retired detectives who had begun the investigation of Shier in 1962. The detective did not want to speak with me directly, but he authorized the intermediary to pass on his recollections. (Because this information is at best third hand, I cannot be certain about either the dates or the circumstances surrounding Shier's early criminal history. The police department's official records of the case, including the detectives' notes from their conversations with my stepfather, were destroyed, along with other inactive records from that time.) The officer informed me about the botched operations at the hospital in Toronto and the sodomy charge in Colorado, gave me the approximate dates, and confirmed that the investigation had ended soon after it began because Shier had fled the state. The detective also recalled that Shier might have been killed shortly after he left California, possibly in South America, but he could not remember precisely.

In 1989, years before this conversation with the LAPD officer took place, I interviewed Evelyn Carrothers at her home in Studio City about her experiences with Shier. She said that "behind a façade of solicitous concern", Shier was a "mean man". A bully. She had never liked him, she said, but he had been very successful treating alcoholics in the Los Angeles area in the 1950s, and she herself had referred many people to him over the years. At the time I spoke with her, Evelyn had not only been sober a long while but had become a prominent member of Alcoholics Anonymous in southern California. She was upset, I thought, by my revelation that Shier was a pedophile, but she wouldn't give me the names of anyone who might have known him. She said she never knew what became of him, but she was sure he was dead. She even argued a case for Shier: Whatever wrong he might have done in his private life, he had been of great value to the larger community.

I've never been able to comprehend Evelyn's sense of the larger good, though her point of view is a position people commonly take when confronted with evidence of sexual crimes committed by people they respect. (A reputation for valued service and magnanimous gestures often forms part of the protective cover pedophiles create.)

A more obvious question I asked myself as I grew older was: How could my mother not have known? Perhaps she did, although she died, a few years after she was told, unwilling to discuss her feelings about what had gone on in California. I've made some measure of peace with her stance. When certain individuals feel severely threatened – emotionally, financially, physically – the lights on the horizon they use to orient themselves in the world might easily wink out. Life can then become a series of fear-driven decisions and compulsive acts of self-protection. People start to separate what is deeply troubling in their lives from what they see as good. To use the usual metaphor, they isolate the events from one another by storing them in different rooms in a large hotel. While these rooms share a corridor, they do not communicate directly with one another.

I'm not able, today, to put the image I have of my mother as her children's attentive guardian together with the idea of her as an innocent, a person blinded by the blandishments of a persistent pedophile. But for whatever reason, she was not able, back then, to consider what might be happening in the hours after she saw Shier drive away, her son's head, from her point of view on the porch, not quite clearing the sill of the car window as the two of them departed.

In June 1970, my stepfather related to my mother, without my knowledge, a distorted and incomplete version of what her friend Harry Shier had done, breaking the promise he had made to me that day eight years before when I'd spoken to him. They were having lunch together in Midtown Manhattan; she became hysterical and was taken from the restaurant by ambulance to a hospital. When she called me that evening, all she could bring herself to say, in a voice resigned and defeated, was, "I know what happened. I know what happened to you."

And then she never spoke of it again.

Six years later, in July 1976, as my mother was dying of lung cancer. I asked her whether she wanted to speak to me about California. She lay on her bed in a private room at Manhattan's Lenox Hill Hospital, rocking her head slowly back and forth like a metronome. Her face averted, she wept silently while I sat mute in a chair by the bed. She would not take my hand. Some of the pathways of a debilitating sexual history are simply destined never to be mapped.

The reasons monstrously abusive relationships persist between people are as complex, I think, as the mathematics of turbulence. The explanation I gave myself for decades, partly to avoid having to address any question of my own complicity, was that I had done this in order to keep our family safe and intact. After my father abandoned us, my mother told me that I would now be the man of the house. I took her remark literally. I began to double-check the locks on the doors at night. I mowed and weeded the lawn and took the trash out to the incinerator in the back yard to burn. I got the day's mail from the box on the street. Whenever Shier showed up at the door, I would bear down on myself: Just see the business with Shier through, I said to myself. Maybe another man, one of the more likable men Mother dated, would come and stay with us. And this one wouldn't walk out. Standing in the shower in Shier's filthy apartment, washing the blood and semen off my legs, I hammered this thought into my mind: You cannot quit. I bottled the anger. I hid the blood. I adamantly focused anywhere else.

What my stepfather actually did when he went to California in 1962, and how he presented Shier's crimes to the detectives, I will never know. And though I know he saw Evelyn at that time, I don't know what he discussed with her. Over the years, right up to his death, whenever I asked him about what he'd done, he became evasive. In an effort to seem sincere, he would occasionally recall a forgotten detail from one of his conversations with the detectives. This additional fact would sometimes shift my basic understanding of the longer story he had already told, raising new questions. Or, alternatively, trying to demonstrate compassion, he might suddenly recall a fact meant to soothe me but that made no sense. He told me once, for example, that during his 1962 visit Evelyn had taken him to see Shier's grave at the Forest Lawn Memorial-Park in Glendale – several weeks before Shier was supposedly killed in an out-of-state automobile accident.

My stepfather, a recovering alcoholic, became, like Evelyn, a regionally prominent figure in Alcoholics Anonymous in the late 1960s. Whenever I inquired, in those early weeks of the investigation, about what sort of progress the detectives were making, he would find a way to mention how many alcoholics Shier had helped. Alcoholism, he said, was a "terrible disease", a more pervasive and serious issue, he wanted me to understand, than pedophilia. He suggested I would benefit from a slightly different perspective on all this. Shier, he conceded, was an awful man – but he had done a lot of good. I should consider, instead, how well I was doing. At 17 I was student-body president at my Jesuit prep school. I had the highest academic average in my class senior year; I was lettering in two sports; I was escorting debutantes to balls at the Plaza, the Sherry-Netherland, the Pierre. Whatever might have occurred in California, he said, things had actually worked out all right. I should let it go.

For 30 years this was exactly the path I chose. Silence. I believed that in spite of Shier's brutalizations I could develop a stable, productive life, that I could simply walk away from everything that had happened.

The conclusion I eventually reached about my stepfather's refusal to pursue charges against Shier was that he did not want the family to be embarrassed by a trial. He was unable to understand that the decision to face cross-examination in a courtroom was not his to make. He could not appreciate that the opportunity to stand up in a public forum and describe, with Shier present, what he had done, and what he had forced me to do, was as important to me as any form of legal justice. Not to be allowed to speak or, worse, to have someone else relate my story and write its ending was to extend the original, infuriating experience of helplessness, to underscore the humiliation of being powerless. My stepfather's ultimate dismissal of my request for help was an instance, chilling for me, of an observation that victims of child molestation often make: If you tell them, they won't believe you. Believing you entails too much disruption.

From what I have read over the years in newspapers and magazines about scandals involving serial pedophiles, I have gathered that people seem to think that what victims most desire in the way of retribution is money and justice, apparently in that order. My own guess would be that what they most want is something quite different: they want to be believed, to have a foundation on which they can rebuild a sense of dignity. Reclaiming self-respect is more important than winning money, more important than exacting vengeance.

Victims do not want someone else's public wrath, the umbrage of an attorney or an editorial writer or a politician, to stand in for the articulation of their own anger. When a pedophile is exposed by a grand-jury indictment today, the tenor of public indignation often seems ephemeral to me, a response generated by "civic" emotion. Considering the number of children who continue to be abused in America — something like one in seven boys and one in three girls — these expressions of condemnation seem naïve. Without a deeper commitment to vigilance, society's outrage begins to take on the look of another broken promise.

Up until the time I interviewed Evelyn in the late 1980s, I had grown to more or less accept my stepfather's views about what had happened in California — which was, of course, my own form of denial. Whatever had been done to me, I held to the belief that things had actually turned out fairly well. By the time I was 40 I had experienced some national success as a writer. I was friends with a large, if geographically scattered, group of people. And I was living happily in a rural, forested area in western Oregon with my wife of 20 years. Significantly, since I had moved to this mountainous place in 1970, the emotional attachment I felt to my home had become essential to any ongoing sense of well-being I had. My almost daily contact there with wild animals, the physical separation of the house from the homes of my neighbors, the flow of a large white-water river past the property, the undomesticated land unfolding for miles around, the rawness of the weather at the back door — all of it fed a feeling of security.

During the years of "traumatic sexual abuse", the term psychologists use for serial sexual abuse, the deepest and sometimes only relief I had was when I was confronted with the local, elementary forces of nature: hot Santa Ana winds blowing west into the San Fernando Valley from the Mojave Desert; Pacific storm surf crashing at Zuma and the other beaches west of Malibu; winter floods inundating our neighborhood when Caballero Creek breached its banks on its way to the Los Angeles River. I took from each of these encounters a sense of what it might feel like to become fully alive. When I gazed up beneath a flock of homing birds or listened as big winds swirled the dry leaves of eucalyptus trees or sat alone somewhere in a rarely traversed part of the Santa Monica Mountains, waiting for a glimpse of a coyote or a brush rabbit, I would feel exhilaration. Encouragement.

But deep inside, I knew things remained awry. (It is relatively easy today — it wasn't then — to find pertinent and explicit information about childhood sexual trauma. How one interprets that information or chooses to act on it remains a perilous second step.) I could not, for example, shake the old thought that by not having acted sooner I was somehow responsible for what happened to other boys after I left California. According to my stepfather, one of the investigating detectives said I had been lucky to walk away in 1956. Continuing their investigation after Shier disappeared, my stepfather told me, the detectives had located three other boys, "none of whom had fared well". The detectives' advice to my stepfather had been that neither he nor I should inquire further into what Harry Shier had been doing with young boys during his years in North Hollywood.

When I began a deliberate inquiry into my past, starting in 1989, I thought of myself as a man walking around with shrapnel sealed in his flesh, and I wanted to get the fragments out. The doubts and images I had put aside for years were now starting to fester. I felt more or less continually seasick, confronting every day a harrowing absence within myself. I imagined it as a mineshaft of bleak, empty space, which neither the love of a spouse nor the companionship of friends nor professional success could efface. The thought began to work on me that a single, bold step, however, some sort of confrontation with the past, might sufficiently jar this frame of mind and change it. I could, I thought, dramatically cure myself in this way.

I phoned Forest Lawn Memorial-Park. No, there was no Harry Shier buried in any of their cemeteries. I couldn't find an obituary for him in any of the southern California papers either. I called Evelyn and asked whether I could come to California and interview her. I would begin my healing, my ablution, by speaking with someone who had known him well. And on that same trip, I decided, I'd drive the rental car to 12003 Riverside Drive in North Hollywood. If the sanitarium was still there, I'd walk through the front door.

Shier's rooftop apartment, nearly hidden behind the branches of several Norfolk Island pines, remained just visible from the sidewalk. I parked in the shade of a pepper tree on Ben Street and walked through the main entrance of the white stucco building, which now housed a private secondary school, a yeshiva. No one took any notice of me standing in the foyer. If someone had come up to inquire about my business, I was prepared to say that I had been a patient in this place 30 years earlier, when it had been a hospital. But I seemed to be invisible.

I walked down the main corridor. In rooms to my right, where I'd once seen the bedridden lying in dim shadow, lights now blazed. Attentive students sat at desks, avidly scribbling while someone lectured. I arrived at an intersection and suddenly found myself staring at the foot of an interior staircase. The door to the stairs, slightly ajar, revealed steps winding upward to the left. My throat clenched like a fist in my neck.

I left the building as soon as I was able to turn around. I ran across Riverside Drive into an outdoor nursery with a fence around it. I went down a pea-gravel path, past potted camellias and oleanders, past blooming primroses and azaleas. After a few minutes, breathing easily once more, the rigidity gone out of my back muscles, I crossed back to where I'd parked the car and drove away.

Later that afternoon, at the Central Library on West Fifth Street in downtown Los Angeles, I gathered several San Fernando Valley phone books from the 1950s, trying to remember the names of my mother's friends, guessing at the spellings – Emery, Falotico, Ling, Murray – hoping to dislodge a memory, to find a thread to follow. When my right index finger came to Shier's name, it halted there below the stark typeface. My bowels burst into my trousers.

In the men's room, I threw my undershorts into a waste bin and washed my pants in the sink, trying to keep the wet spot small. I was in my stocking feet, putting my pants back on, when a guard entered abruptly and stood alert and suspicious in the doorway. He informed me that the library was closing. I'll be only another moment, I assured him.

A few minutes later, shielding the wet seat of my pants with my briefcase, I met a friend for dinner nearby. When the maître d' asked whether we preferred eating outdoors or in, I suggested we sit outside. I didn't tell my friend where I'd been that day.

Over the years, I'd spoken to very few people about Shier – my brother, serious girlfriends, my wife, a few close friends. I didn't feel any need to be heard, and the chance of being misunderstood, of being taken for no more than the innocent victim, long ago, of a criminal's heinous acts seemed great. Pity, I thought, would take things in the wrong direction for me. What I wanted to know now was: What happened to me?

In the months following my visit to the building on Riverside, I placed an occasional call to state and county agencies in California, trying to track down some of the details that might have framed my story. Doing this, I came to suspect that I was missing the memory of certain events. I could recall many scenes from my childhood in the Valley, even remember some vividly; but I also became aware of gaps in that period of time from which nothing surfaced.

In the fall of 1996, I visited a therapist for the first time. I'd briefly seen a psychiatrist when I was in college, but we were not able to get anywhere. Years later, I understood it was because I hadn't been capable at the time of doing the required work. My expectation was that she would somehow simply fix me, get me over the anxiety, over the humiliation.

I chose therapy because my own efforts to clarify my past seemed dramatically unproductive, and because I was now, once again, of a mind that something was wrong with me. I had begun to recognize patterns in my behavior. If I sensed, for example, that I was being manipulated by someone, or disrespected, I quickly became furious out of all proportion. And I'd freeze sometimes when faced with a serious threat instead of calmly moving toward some sort of resolution. I suspected that these habits – no great insight – were rooted in my childhood experience.

Also, a persistent, anxiety-induced muscular tension across my shoulders had by now become so severe that I'd ruptured a cervical disc. When a regimen of steroids brought only limited relief, my doctor recommended surgery. After a second doctor said I had no option but surgery, I reluctantly agreed – until the surgical procedure was drawn up for me on a piece of paper: I'd be placed facedown and unconscious on an operating table, and a one-inch vertical slit would be opened in the nape of my neck. I said no, absolutely not. I'd live with the pain.

From the beginning, the therapist encouraged me to move at my own pace through the memories I was able to retrieve, and to resist the urge to fit any of these events into a pattern. I remember him saying in one of our first sessions, with regard to my apparent inability to protect myself in complex emotional situations such as my stepfather's betrayal, that I did "not even understand the concept of self-protection". I resented the statement. It made me feel stupid – but it also seemed like a start.

We worked together for four years. I described for him the particulars of the abuse: the sandpaper burn of Shier's evening stubble on my skin; his antic Chihuahua, which defecated on the floor of the apartment and raced around on the bed when we were in it; Shier's tongue jammed into my mouth. I described the time he forced me to perform fellatio in my home while my mother and brother were away. Shier lay back on Mother's sleeping couch, self-absorbed, palming my head like a melon, supremely at ease. I told the therapist about my inability to break off the relationship with Shier, and about my mother's apparent intention to look the other way.

At the start of therapy, I speculated that the real horror of those years would prove to be the actual acts of abuse – my choking on his semen, the towel forced over my face to silence me, the rectal bleeding. After a while, I began to see that the horror was more elusive, that it included more than just betrayals and denials and being yanked around in Shier's bed like a rag doll. The enduring horror was that I had learned to accommodate brutalization. This part of the experience remained with me long after I walked out of Shier's apartment for the last time.

Caught up in someone else's psychosis, overmatched at every turn, I had concentrated on only one thing: survival. To survive I needed to placate. My response to emotional confrontation in the years following that time, I came to see, was almost always to acquiesce, or to overreact angrily, with no option in between. Therapy led me to comprehend that I had not, as I wanted to believe, been able to tough out the trauma. I had succumbed, and others besides me had experienced the consequences of my attempt to endure. I had ahead of me now a chance to do better, to be a person less given to anger.

I visited the therapist twice a week to start with, occasionally for double sessions; then it was once a week or less frequently until we decided we'd come to a resting place. In our final sessions, I fitted the pieces of my story together differently, creating "another narrative", as therapists are wont to say, of the early years in California, a broader context for the physical and emotional damage. After that, long-term sexual abuse no longer organized the meaning of my life as it had during the years I believed that I'd simply walked away from it.

One night in 1998, driving from the town where I had been seeing the therapist 40 miles upriver to my home, I suddenly felt flooded with relief. The sensation was so strong I pulled over and got out of the truck. I walked to the edge of what I knew to be an unfenced, cultivated field. At first I thought I was experiencing physical relief, the breakdown of the last bit of tension in my upper back, which, after many weeks of physical therapy, no longer required surgery. But it was something else. A stony, overbearing presence I'd been fearful of nearly all my life wasn't there anymore. I stood in the dark by the side of the road for a long while, savoring the reprieve, the sudden disappearance of this tyranny. I recalled a dream I'd had midway through my therapy. I burst through a heavy cellar door and surprised an ogre devouring the entrails of a gutted infant, alive but impassive in the grip of his hand. The ogre was enraged at being discovered. What seemed significant was that I had broken down the door. It didn't matter whether it was the door into something or the door out.

Therapy's success for me was not so much my coming to understand that I had learned as a child to tolerate acts of abuse. It was discovering a greater capacity within myself to empathize with another person's nightmare. Most of the unresolved fear and anger I once held on to has now metamorphosed into compassion, an understanding of the predicaments nearly everyone encounters, at some level, at some time, in their lives.

A commonplace about trauma, one buried deep in the psyches of American men, is that it is noble to heal alone. What I've learned in recent years, however, is that this choice sometimes becomes a path to further isolation and trouble, especially for the family and friends of the one who has been wounded. I took exactly this path, intending to bother no one with my determined effort to recalibrate my life. It took a long while for me to understand that a crucial component of recovery from trauma is learning to comprehend and accept the embrace of someone who has no specific knowledge of what happened to you, who is disinterested.

We need others to bring us back into the comity of human life. This appears to have been the final lesson for me – to appreciate someone's embrace not as forgiveness or as an amicable judgment but as an acknowledgment that, from time to time, private life becomes brutally hard for every one of us, and that without one another, without some sort of community, the nightmare is prone to lurk, waiting for an opening.

I'm not interested any longer in tracking down the details of Harry Shier's death, or in wondering how, if it is still there, I might reenter his apartment above the building on Riverside Drive to gaze out at the sky through the corner window. I'm on the alert, now, though, for an often innocuous moment, the one in which an adult man begins to show an unusual interest in the welfare of someone's young son – especially if it's my grandson. He still, at the age of nine, reaches out for my hand when we start to cross a dangerous street.

Barry Lopez was born in 1945, and grew up in New York and California. An essayist, author, fiction-writer and landscape photographer, he is widely considered one of the premier nature-writers in the United States, whose work across several genres is renowned for its ethical, environmental and humanitarian concerns. He is the author of nine volumes of fiction, most recently Resistance *(Knopf, 2004), as well as six works of non-fiction, most famously* Arctic Dreams: Imagination and Desire in a Northern Landscape *(Scribner's, 1986). He now lives in Oregon.*

TWA POEMS

Andrew Philip

MID ACHIN', A HILL, A PIPE

An abnominal for Aidan Michael Philip

Ma ainlie laddie, male meme
in ma clan; alpha in child line;

name hidden in mine. Handed
a damned deal: nae medic lanced

an ill in him. Nae pill, nae needle,
nae chalice healed

a dampened DNA chain.
Daddied, I claimed him hail.

I held him, palm in palm.
I named him. Mama called him

and he apened limpid een.
Mama hand and mine cleaned

him. He ailed me. Pain and pride
meld in ma manchild

happed deep, laid in land alane.
Ach – I parade a candid ache.

Maimed, I acclaim him
acme *mac*, ee-aipple, dim

peace candle. Hidden laddie
hained, clenched, clad in me.

Scots glosses:
ma my; *ainlie* only; *laddie* boy; *nae* no; *hail* whole; *apened* opened; *een* eyes;
happed closed, concealed; *alane* alone; *mac* (Gaelic) son; *ee-aipple* eye-apple;
hained enclosed, protected, preserved

ENIGMA DROWN

An abnominal for Edwin Morgan

O ion-engined man
grown in a Weegie room;

engineer o an android ream;
winning one-man Armada agin

arid, ingrained meme; winged
daemon and *imago dei* in

a rearranged marriage;
diner on good word marrow;

dreamer o a new mode, a new *mondo*;
mariner on meaning margin —

I am awed again and again.
Am I a worm and no man

agin our non-grand grandee,
warm grandad o *dàin agam*?

No. I read and emerged
growing in a wilder garden,

reading in *Error!* a gain —
an ore, a grain o gowd.

O arrow o origin, O modern gong –
I owe an ode in memoriam.

Scots glosses:
Weegie Glaswegian; *agin* against; *dàin agam* (Gaelic) my poems; *gowd* gold

Abnominal: a form developed by the author, using only the letters of the dedicatee's name, each of which must appear at least once per stanza.

Andrew Philip was born in Aberdeen in 1975 and grew up near Falkirk. His first full collection of poetry, dealing with a bereavement, The Ambulance Box *(Salt, 2009), was shortlisted for the Aldeburgh First Collection Prize and the Seamus Heaney Centre Prize for Poetry. His second collection,* The North End of the Possible, *is due out from Salt in 2013. He now lives in Linlithgow, and is one of the two Scots Language Editors of this journal.*

POEM

—

Dorothy Lawrenson

A HIND'S DAUGHTER

Miles from the kailyard I tracked her down,
just after the war. *What was it like?*
I asked her, and *what was he like?*
— but so much had happened since then.

... *Sae ah went intae service and merried a groom*
— onything tae get awa fae the ferm!
I heard of her son's death at Arras,
and of Glasgow's bombed out houses —

Wis ah gled tae see the back o thae slums!
The hinds raw wis nae palace, ye ken,
but ye could aye see daylicht. Jings!
— whit wis that ye wur askin me, hen?

The airtist? Oh, he wis aye pesterin
me to pose oot there in the gairden.
Faither wis sweir tae allow it — that is, till
Guthrie gied him a gift in the shape o a bottle.

Aw the long cauld efternin he pentit
and ah'd tae stand like this — she demonstrates
in her paisley apron, with a kitchen knife for a gully,
her cropped hair the China white of the November sky.

Scots glosses:
hind a married, skilled farmworker; *kailyard* cabbage garden; *ah* I; *merried*
married; *onything* anything; *awa* away; *ferm* farm; *gled* glad; *thae* those; *hinds*
raw row of cottages occupied by farmworkers; *ken* know; *aye* always; *daylicht*

daylight; *jings* expletive; *whit* what; *hen* affectionate or familiar form of address for a girl or woman; *sweir* reluctant, unwilling; *gied* gave; *aw* all; *cauld* cold; *efternin* afternoon; *pentit* painted; *gully* large knife

Dorothy Lawrenson is an artist and graphic designer from Dundee. Her poems have been published in Gutter, *as well as a number of other Scottish journals. She is the author of two pamphlets,* Under the Threshold *(2005) and* The Year *(2012), both from Perjink. She now lives in Edinburgh.*

FOWER POEMS

—

Aonghas MacNeacail

ANE BROWNSBANK VEESIT

gin ye bide but ae nicht
in yon wee ludge
ye'll hear the ghaist
o a risp in the vyce o
an auld keeng in his
ain maikless republic

leuk at thae waws – ane
gailerie o seein-glesses
whaur thon auld baird
coud tak tent o ilka
pictur o his sel, guid
freends haed makkit

sleep weel, gin chris
disna insist oan threapin
wi ye anent the wey ye'd
ettle tae scrieve a verse –
tho ye hae tae mind he's
but a ghaist, a ghaist nou

anely a ghaist – bit he'd
        like ye tae ken

Scots glosses:
brownsbank Hugh MacDiarmid's cottage; *veesit* visit; *gin* if; *bide* stay; *ae*
one; *nicht* night; *yon* that; *wee* little; *ludge* lodge; *ghaist* ghost; *risp* harsh
grating sound; *vyce* voice; *auld* old; *keeng* king; *ain* own; *maikless*
matchless; *leuk* look; *thae* those; *waws* walls; *ane* a; *gailerie* gallery;

seein-glesses mirrors; *whaur* where; *thon* that; *baird* bard; *tak tent* pay attention; *ilka* every; *pictur* picture; *his sel* himself; *guid* good; *freends* friends; *haed* had; *makkit* made; *weel* well; *disna* does not; *oan* on; *threapin wi ye* arguing with you; *anent* about; *wey* way; *ettle tae screive* attempt to write; *hae* have; *mind* remember; *nou* now; *anely* only; *bit* but; *ken* know

DRUMMIN

the wey thon chiel wis drummin
at the winnock ye micht think he
haed a deevil chowin at his airse
whan aw it wis wis aggie wantin
tae hae wards wi him anent neist
friday's speicial prayer meetin in
the auld heich covenantin kirk at
whilk she's mindit tae mak goad
ane paction for his wandert saul

he didna hae tae sclim the yett
atween hissel an her for thon —
he's nae sae coorse a sinner as
she's meisurit: her ane gless ee
wis niver awthegither biblical —
warld, flesh, deevil, still his wale
or ettlin for his ane douce airt —
bit och, that ee aye follaes him
an he's nae boun for hainin yet

Scots glosses:
wey way; *thon* that; *chiel* young man, fellow; *winnock* window; *micht* might; *haed* had; *deevil* devil; *chowin* chewing; *airse* arse; *whan* when; *aw* all; *wis* was; *wards* words; *wi* with; *anent* about; *neist* next; *auld* old; *heich* high; *covenantin* supporting the National Covenant of 1638 and/or the Solemn League and Covenant of 1643; *kirk* church; *whilk*

which; *mak* make; *goad* God; *ane paction* a bargain; *wandert saul* wandered soul; *didna* did not; *sclim* climb; *yett* gate; *atween* between; *hissel* himself; *nae sae coorse a sinner* not so wicked a sinner; *meisurit* measured, reckoned; *ane gless ee* one glass eye; *awthegither* altogether; *warld* world; *wale* choice; *ettlin for his ane douce airt* taking as his objective his own sweet way; *aye* always; *follaes* follow; *nae* not; *boun* bound; *hainin* salvation

KING OR TRAIVELLER

as fowk forgaithert here thegither,
while him they cry the keeng sits
easy wi his freens the traivellers,
aa heeze a gless tae hermonie —
he says he wants a wicelike joab
an no jist hae tae waff his haund
at thae he bygaes in his caur —

aye, richt, but gin he disnae, than
let us inveet him nou tae gie the
thocht some sarious avizandum
an no tae tak ower lang anent it

there's a rowth o joabs that want
the daein, nane sae regal as might
fit a chiel sae fremd fae hivy darg
but shairly, in-thegither, we coud
find ane needfu stent his docht
micht ser as propine tae the maist

an gie him pleisance rich eneuch
tae skare his gear and graith wi aw

Scots glosses:
traiveller traveller; *fowk* folk; *forgaithert* assembled, congregated;
thegither together; *cry* call; *keeng* king; *wi* with; *freens* friends; *aa* all;
heeze lift; *gless* glass; *hermonie* harmony; *wicelike* sensible, reasonable;
joab job; *no jist* not just; *waff his haund* with his hand; *thae he bygaes in
his caur* those he passes in his car; *aye* yes; *richt* right; *gin* if; *disnae* does
not; *inveet* invite; *nou* now; *gie* give; *thocht* thought; *sarious* serious;
avizandum further consideration; *no tae tak ower lang anent it* not to take
too long about it; *rowth* abundance; *want the daein* want done; *nane*
none; *chiel* fellow; *sae fremd frae hivy darg* so unused to heavy work;
shairly surely; *in-thegither* all together; *needfu stent* necessary task; *docht*
strength, ability; *ser* serve; *propine* gift, benefit; *maist* most, majority;
pleisance satisfaction; *eneuch* enough; *skare* share; *gear and graith* wealth
and goods; *aw* all

YON DAY

mind yon day we sclimmed the ben
an leukit oot til the lift's faur easins —
oot ayont
        collogue an weary darg ablo,
ower heich tae hear whit puir humanity
wis coontin —
        stanes, banes or foostit breid
or juist tuim howp
             nae crust or core

an thare we stuid
        licht as a leaf
on its tapmaist stem, an
        heicher even than ilka laverock
cairryin throu its whitter an chirl

oorsels able tae wiss
for a speal whaur we maun pree
a warld whaur aw mey
                    birl on the lift
as lowse as the laverock
singin the sangs
                    dowie or vieve
it can bigg intil ane yairn, plaidit
wi aw it ettles tae mynd or dream

an stowin its thrapple whauriver
thare's an airtin oot o a farin —
pickle o ait or bere,
                an ilk in its season
hyndberry, brammle, buckie or blae
tae hae eneuch, eneuch
is aw

an this, fae oor heich
                plattie o stane, gies aw
the kittilt thochts
                oor deezie harns coud hap
the weenth o aw that lies
                ayont the lift

Scots glosses:

yon that; *mind* remember; *sclimmed* climbed; *ben* mountain; *leukit oot* looked out; *til* to; *the lift's faur easins* the far horizon; *ayont* beyond; *collogue an weary darg ablo* conversation and weary toil below; *ower heich* too high; *whit* what; *puir* poor; *coontin* counting; *stanes* stones; *banes* bones; *foostit breid* mouldy bread; *juist tuim howp* just empty hope; *stuid* stood; *licht* light; *tapmaist* topmost; *ilka* every; *laverock* skylark; *whitter an chirl* twitter and chirp; *oorsels* ourselves; *wiss* wish; *speal* climb; *maun pree* must taste; *warld* world;, *whaur* where; *aw* all; *mey* may; *birl* whirl, twist, turn; *lift* sky; *lowse* loose, free; *sangs* songs; *dowie or vieve* sad or lively; *bigg* build; *yairn* yarn; *plaidit* dressed; *ettles* intends, attempts; *stowin its thrapple* showing its throat; *whauriver thare's an airtin oot o a farin* wherever food is discovered by searching; *pickle o ait or bere* grain of oat or barley; *ilk* each; *hyndberry* wild raspberry; *brammle* bramble; *buckie* rosehip; *blae* bilberry; *eneuch* enough; *plattie* ledge; *gies* gives; *kittilt* stirred up; *deezie* dozy; *harns* brains; *hap* conceal; *weenth* width

See p. 146 for Paddy Bushe's poem on Aonghas MacNeacail.

A Scots Gaelic speaker, and one of the foremost contemporary poets in the three tongues of Scotland, Aonghas MacNeacail was born in Uig, Isle of Skye, in 1942. He was educated locally, before taking a degree from University of Glasgow. He is the author of six collections of poetry: An Seachnadh/The Avoiding *(Macdonald, 1986),* Rock and Water: Poems in English *(Polygon, 1990),* Oideachadh Ceart/A Proper Schooling *(Polygon, 1996),* Laoidh an Donais Oig/Hymn to a Young Demon *(Polygon, 2007), and a new and selected poems in Gaelic,* Deanamh Gàire ris a Chleoc/Laughing at the Clock *(Polygon, 2012). A pamphlet of poems in Scots,* Ayont the Dyke/Beyond the Wall, *is forthcoming. His songs have been set to music by some of Scotland's leading composers and recorded by many well-known singers (a collection of which is also forthcoming). He now lives in the Scottish Borders.*

A WOUNDED LYNX

Eibhear Walshe

Time, again, for some savage indignation?

On the Grand Canal by Charlemont Street, across from a large, brand-new hotel, is a memorial to the Irish novelist Paul Smith. A tiny concrete path leads you off the pavement to what looks like a gravestone set right by the canal. The inscription on the memorial tablet records his name, the date of his birth and death, and the fact that he grew up nearby. It reads:

Paul Smith
Author of *The Countrywoman* and *Esther's Altar*
4th October 1920–11th January 1997
lived opposite this spot.

Underneath, the memorial tablet carries these eight lines of poetry, the opening stanzas from "The Return" by Edna St Vincent Millay:

Earth does not understand her child
Who from the loud, gregarious town
Returns, depleted and defiled,
To the still woods, to fling down.
Earth cannot count the sons she bore:
The wounded lynx, the wounded man
Come trailing blood unto her door;
She shelters both as best she can.

Sometimes, while searching for one thing, along the way you can get lucky with something else, some unexpected find, but this only becomes clear much later. When I started researching for a biography on Kate O'Brien in early 1992, I began by interviewing her friend the retired academic Professor Lorna Reynolds, who had also written a study of O'Brien's fictions. In the course of our conversation, she mentioned that the Irish novelist Paul Smith had known O'Brien very well and that he was now living back in Dublin after many years of working abroad. With her characteristic helpfulness and efficiency, Lorna Reynolds put me in touch with him and so, on a warm July afternoon in 1992, I found myself knocking at the door of Paul Smith's house in Blackrock. At that point, I knew very little about him but I had heard about his novels from stray sources. I even had a copy of one of his novels, *Summer Sang in Me*, on my bookshelf; but I'm sorry to say that I hadn't actually read it before meeting him. In the late 1980s a student of mine in an evening class on the English novel had mentioned to me that Smith's novel *The Countrywoman* was a great favourite of hers. She urged me to read it and to disregard the slightly salacious front cover of a scantily clad woman on the only existing edition available at that point. I didn't read it but, later that year, a friend of mine living in a flat in Portobello in Dublin by the Grand Canal, told me that Paul Smith had grown up around that area, in a now-demolished tenement off Charlemont Street. My friend had read all of Smith's novels and he gave me a present of his favourite one, *Summer Sang in Me*. I have that copy before me as I write. On the cover, it has a side profile of a beautiful young woman with tumbling unkempt hair, naked and covering her breast with her arms, an image totally unconnected with any of the themes of the novel, but, presumably, reflecting the slightly scandalous status of the book as a banned novel.

The evening before I made my visit to Paul Smith in July 1992, I prepared my questions on Kate O'Brien and, at one point, I did take down my copy of *Summer Sang in Me* from my bookshelf. I still hadn't read it, but at least I did read the cover and the biographical note and gleaned some basic background information. Smith's first novel, *Esther's Altar*, a Dublin tenement novel set during the Easter Rising of 1916, had been published in 1959 to great critical acclaim, and he went on to write four more novels, all well received in Ireland and the US. The back cover of my copy of *Summer Sang in Me* carries a quote from Kate O'Brien, who wrote, "It went straight home to one's central nerves." (She was right. When I did finally read it, it made exactly that impression, not exactly comfortable or enjoyable but compelling and unforgettable.) Below that, there is also a quote from, of all people, Dorothy Parker, who had written of Smith in *Esquire*, "I realise that to put a writer's name on the same page as that of Sean O'Casey is giddy high praise. But now I think it is time for it." All of this should have made me more curious to read him, but Kate O'Brien was my main focus that summer and for a while to come.

In the biographical note on the fly-page of the novel, Paul Smith writes of himself in this way: "I was born and raised in Dublin in a house near a bridge spanning a canal. My education was rather do-it-yourself. To this day I cannot recite the alphabet or multiplication tables. I have always done what I wanted to do and never cared what others thought. As an artist and an individual my impulse has always been to move on. I learned to read at pre-school age. I began writing in my twenties." Therefore, I was more than a little surprised, given this childhood, when I did meet him on that July day to discover that he had a pronounced English accent. (As it happened, this Eliza Doolittle-like transformation of his accent was something that Smith was refreshingly honest about. In an interview in the *Sunday Tribune* in 1987, he told the reporter that, as a teenager, auditioning for work in Dublin's Gate Theatre, Hilton Edwards and Micheál MacLiammóir took him aside sympathetically. "The first thing if you want to come into this world", advised MacLiammóir, "if you want to work in theatre, if you want to do anything at all in Dublin, get rid of that voice. That has to go if you do anything at all." Smith went on to say that, for him, "the transition was enormous, suddenly finding yourself with books, all round the place, music that you'd never heard before. I changed everything. The way I dressed, the way I thought, the way I spoke.")

When I met him that afternoon, he was a lean-looking man with a florid complexion, trim and healthy-looking for his 72 years, well dressed in a casual blue wool jumper and brown cords. Quiet and self-contained in manner, he brought me into his study, a room as neat and trim as himself, with an old typewriter on the desk and books on every shelf, and offered me some tea. To begin with, I found him more than a little intimidating, although he was polite and welcoming in terms of conversation. There was something in his expression, a reserve, with a slightly resentful air, wary and measured in his answers to my questions, as if he expected some confrontation between us. I tried to find common ground by mentioning my great interest in Margaret Burke Sheridan, whose biography he had on his desk. "Yes, Maggie", he answered in a slightly dreamy tone. "She had the most luminous blue eyes I've ever seen." When I talked about my interest in all his vanished friends of 1950s bohemian Dublin, MacLiammóir, Edwards, Kate O'Brien, he thawed somewhat and began talking about the Kate O'Brien Lecture in Limerick, a lecture that was described in *The Irish Times* as "forceful and provocative", and he was unhappy with some of the local reactions to his memories of Kate O'Brien. He told me about the confrontation that had ensued, but I got the impression that he was a man unafraid of confrontation. He said that he still travelled between Ireland and

Los Angeles and was still adapting stories for the stage. Indeed, at one point, he excused himself to answer the phone, a brief conversation with a few monosyllables on his side, and when he returned he told me that his publishers were pushing him to finish off a stage adaptation. (At the time, I wondered if that was just a fiction for my benefit, an unworthy thought, but later I discovered that one of his novels had indeed been adapted for stage in Los Angeles.)

As we talked, he became less wary and opened up about Kate O'Brien, someone he clearly loved and admired, with an unsentimental honesty. He talked about her drinking and about the vicissitudes of her personal life and what came across most was his affectionate appreciation of her humour and her intellect. He drew my attention to a pencil portrait of O'Brien by one of the partners, the artist Mary O'Neill, a legacy from Kate herself, sitting on his bookshelf next to an old hardback volume, the poems of Edna St Vincent Millay. I've always wondered where it ended up. Finally, he came to what seemed to him to be the crucial point about Kate O'Brien. He told me that it was important for me to acknowledge that she was lesbian and he talked about four Englishwomen, all of them O'Brien's lovers, and all of great significance in her life. Eventually, when I had finally completed my researches in Britain, I found that Smith had been accurate in each case. He was one of the first people I interviewed about her and I was very new to the process of biographical research, and therefore, I had no way of evaluating his memories in terms of reliability. In the course of many later interviews, I learned, the hard way, about the validity of some remembrances. The less some of my interviewees actually knew her, the more they invented and, later, when I went to check these memories against surviving documentary evidence, they proved elusive or unsustainable. When I got the chance to research these women partners by interviewing surviving family in Britain, I found that Paul Smith had been completely reliable in his recollections. (His honesty is also a central feature of his fictions, as I was to discover.) At the end of the afternoon, after about three hours of conversation, he walked me to his garden gate and we parted on very warm terms, his caution gone, and my gratitude for his help evident. Tactfully, he made no mention of the fact that I clearly hadn't read a word of his own writing and had no interest in it, and that I only saw him in relation to his friendship with Kate O'Brien, which must have stung, however slightly. I left him that day, feeling that I had connected directly with a living past, a past that fascinated me, the world of actors, writers and opera divas all living in the Dublin of the 1950s, around the Shelbourne and The Gate Theatre, and I wanted to hear more. The following week, I phoned him again, asking if I could visit and talk more about Kate O'Brien. He refused, sounding cold and unwelcoming on the phone, saying that he had told me all he remembered and had nothing to add. The shutters had gone back up.

Then, over the next year, I began collecting copies of his books, now all out of print, and I was sorry I had failed to do so before meeting him, as his voice was as powerful a lost one for me as Kate O'Brien's had been. I wished I had taken the time to read him that summer and I would have liked to ask him something about his own journey towards creative fulfilment, the boy brought up in a tenement with little education, becoming an actor, teacher and then a popular novelist, celebrated in the US, the friend of writers and actors, the subject of censorship.

In gathering and reading all of his books, I discovered that Smith's great burst of creativity came, unsurprisingly, with his move away from Ireland, given the directness and honesty of his work. In the late 1950s Smith moved to Sweden, teaching at the University of Uppsala and there, in the long Nordic evenings, he wrote his first novel, *Esther's Altar*. He described this first experience of writing in an interview thus: "I never put pen to paper before but I sat down and wrote out of rage." A drama of the Dublin slums set during the week of the 1916 Rising, *Esther's Altar* was published in 1959 to great acclaim. With the success of his first novel, lauded by Dorothy Parker amongst others, Smith moved on to Canada and then to America where, in 1962, he published two more novels, *The Countrywoman* and *The Stubborn Season*. As part of this flood of creativity, the next year saw the publication of his novel *Stravaganza*, four novels in four years; and finally he published a sequel to *The Countrywoman* ten years later in 1972, called *Annie* in the United States and *Summer Sang in Me* in Britain and Ireland. This period of travel clearly gave him the distance to write about Ireland in the honest way that he did, so much so that his books were banned. Then it all stopped. When he moved back to Dublin in 1972, as far as I can tell, he never published another novel. There was a BBC TV version of *Esther's Altar* in 1976, and he worked on a stage adaptation of *The Countrywoman* for Siobhan McKenna, but she died before the play was ready.

The dust jackets on his novels, now all out of print, gave me more and more biographical information as I collected them. *Stravaganza*, my least favourite, has the most interesting dust jacket, with a picture of the 43-year-old Smith, a smiling, handsome, neat-featured man, recognizable to me as an early version of the elderly man I had met, and a quote from Anthony Burgess writing about *The Stubborn Season* in *The Observer*: "Whenever a drunken Dublin writer is a genius I don't feel like committing myself to the word: but I am sorely tempted."

Again and again, each successive novel (with the exception of *Stravaganza*) draws on a similar imaginative world, the darkness of slum life and the struggle to survive in a brutal wounding world, and, of them all, *The Countrywoman* seems to have been the most autobiographical. In an interview, he described how his mother had raised ten children alone on seven shillings and sixpence when his father was away during the First World War fighting with the British Army. His mother, Kate Smith, born O'Brien, was from Wicklow, like the heroine of his novel, Molly Baines, and Smith remembered that his mother "hated the city ... she was absolutely lost in it". *The Countrywoman* is a novel of loss and despair about the damage of the "loud gregarious town", as is the sequel, *Summer Sang in Me*; and, as a pair, these two novels seem to me to be Smith's finest achievement, particularly the second, and his last completed novel. The title comes from a sonnet by Edna St Vincent Millay:

> I cannot say what loves have come and gone,
> I only know that summer sang in me
> A little while, that in me sings no more

It takes place around Portobello in Dublin, where two tenement children, Annie and Tucker Tommy, in their early teens, struggle to earn a living whatever way they can in the slums of Rock Street by the Grand Canal. Annie is full of intelligence and resourcefulness and tries to scrape a bare living by begging from the nearby wealthy houses on Leeson Park and Northbrook Road. Annie, the older of the two and the object of the narrator's hero-worship, works day and night to keep hunger at bay – for example, by combing through the ash-cans left outside the big houses to glean a few cinders to sell on to other tenement neighbours. She dreads being sent to work in a nearby factory. "And with Barker's biscuit factory shadowing her like some creature of nightmares black and terrifying and many-armed, Annie entered upon a new time of waiting."

Tucker Tommy, already a character in his earlier novel *The Countrywoman*, is the narrator here and seems to be an alter-ego for Smith himself. Tucker Tommy loves Annie for her toughness and resourcefulness. In an interview, Smith said about the original for Annie, "All I did was record her – truthfully – the way she would have been had she been around. She was in constant conflict with the fake around her and for the first 12 years of my life, was the one clear centre from which everything went out and to which everything returned." Smith builds the novel around the landscape around the Grand Canal in Dublin in the early 1930s, a landscape dominated by poverty and fear, and written with a kind of unsettling raw sensitivity, punctuated by moments of unexpected tenderness. He said of his childhood, with a certain irony, I suspect, "for people who never knew that life, it may sound absolutely ghastly, but it was magic for a child. It prepared you for what was to come. I think you should either be born very rich or very poor. If you are born between, you don't stand a chance." His writing style is uneven, moments of uncertain lyricism with a grim realist narrative like this surprising moment of homoerotic passion:

> But he chased me, and catching me, Johnny Roscoe kissed me. And that's when it happened and that's how it happened. Just like that up against a wall. No palaver, no nothing. And I told him to "give over". Because I thought he was more serious than he should've been and because I was scared stiff – not of him but of myself and the shock running through my body. And to escape the grip his arms made, and to stop from reaching out for something that, till now, I'd been denied, I started to lash out at the familiar face gone strange with emotion – and then, with a blast of anger, he began to smother my mouth and the sounds of protest I was making with lips that were hard as hell at first – before they went summer soft.

Smith must have been one of the few Irish writers of the working class to dare write about same-sex desire and, not surprisingly, his books were banned. Death is the theme, and the observation of the middle-class life from the perspective of the slum children. Annie and Tommy are like the young Cathy and Heathcliff in *Wuthering Heights* looking in on Thrushcross Grange, when they see a middle-class man hanging in his own garden, a suicide.

> In death, Mr Hogan was a long man: a long man in the grip of some terrible emotion, swaying easily where he hung. I didn't

want to see his eyes but I saw them, fixed on us in black penetration. There was knowledge in his face, a long and painful knowledge, and in the downward slope of the head, a sad pity, sprung from the very foundations of time. Instead of the branches of the tree, the faces of every man, woman and child who had ever been born might have made a backdrop for him, without seeming the least bit strange.

The novel ends in despair and a doomed future for Annie and, as Kate O'Brien suggests, goes straight to the nerves. It is, in my opinion, his best work.

Then, when Smith published a memoir of Kate O'Brien in 1994, in a series of lectures from the Kate O'Brien weekend, I found out a great deal about his friendship with her and a little more about him, albeit a tantalizingly small amount. He explained that he came to know Kate through The Gate's founders, Hilton Edwards and Micheál MacLiammóir: "I first met her when she reappeared in Irish life after the publication of *That Lady* in 1945 and a few years later returned to Ireland … I was invited by Hilton Edwards and Michael MacLiammoir to dinner in 4 Harcourt Terrace and she and Margaret Burke-Sheridan were fellow guests." He was just under 30 when he was invited to that dinner and must have been very good company indeed to hold his own in this high-octane group of fiftysomething opera singers, writers and actors. The journey from Charlemont Street, where he grew up, to that flat in Harcourt Terrace was tiny in terms of distance, but titanic in terms of class; however, Smith managed to fit right into this bohemian world, and he retained the friendships of Sheridan, O'Brien, MacLiammóir and Edwards throughout. The primary friendship was that between O'Brien and Smith, a friendship that lasted despite the great differences between the two. As he wrote, "in a sense, two extremes met in us. She, representative of a prosperous middle-class, conventionally educated, widely travelled, widely experienced, a woman of deep culture, and I, a working-class Dubliner, who had never known where his next cut of bread or next pair of runners was coming from." Describing her as "the most interesting woman I've ever met", Smith was sensitive to her class prejudices and her idealization of the bourgeoisie; "she was a tangled fishnet of contradictions. She liked the rich because she liked the way they spoke." Kate found the friendship of younger men enjoyable, especially if they had literary interests, and she encouraged Paul Smith's writing. Later, his most successful novel, *The Countrywoman*, published in 1962, caused some confusion when he dedicated it to his late mother, who also happened to be called Kate O'Brien. Both O'Brien and Smith had to make it clear that they were not mother and son, perhaps a little embarrassing for O'Brien, 25 years older than him.

Like O'Brien, Smith's work was banned in Ireland and remained so until 1975. He stayed in Roundstone in the summer of 1952, using it as a setting for *Stravaganza*, a novel of bohemian life in Connemara, and this brought him even closer to O'Brien. The novel tells a story of Boola (Roundstone) and of the likeable, witty, hard-drinking, clearly lesbian "Sweet Coz" (O'Brien?) from the perspective of the narrator, a writer, and his American wife, Lee. As Smith wrote in his memoir of O'Brien, "At the time she came to supper in the flat in Fitzwilliam Square which I shared with an American student working in Trinity on a thesis on the Anglo-Irish theatre. When in 1952, my flat mate decided that, in order to get his thesis finished, he had to get away from the distractions of Dublin and retreat to the country, I went with him to a cottage in Roundstone, the village where Kate O'Brien bought a house." Smith spent much of that summer in Kate's company: "On the very evening of our arrival, there was an invitation to a party in her house where she was entertaining, among others, Joyce Grenfell and her husband." Smith also accompanied her to the Dublin production of her novel, *That Lady*, in The Gate Theatre and remembered it as a difficult evening: "At the dress rehearsal the day before, Kate had voiced her objection to the heavy ornamentation the leading lady was giving the part. On the first night, she was to sit white-faced and appalled in her dress circle seat and watch Dublin's answer to Ana De Mendoza exit through the dead-centre, upstage fireplace and hear the audience bellow its gutty laughter." Smith stayed in touch with her after she left Roundstone in 1960 and moved back, penniless, to live in the small Kentish village of Boughton until her death in 1974. "I was there on and off for most of those years, but in 1972 I didn't want to see the drinking anymore. We saw each other of course … and I found Kate's drinking made her dull and repetitive, and she made me sad. I last saw Kate in her house in Boughton in September 1973. The present was grim, the future uncertain. She was a sad lonely woman and she gave me my first concern about age because she talked about the horrors of growing old. She lived alone with her cat and her books and with no visible means of support."

I never met Paul Smith again and he died in January 1997, before my biography of Kate O'Brien was completed. But, with his death, a number of obituaries appeared and so, in this way, much more of his life became known to me. The newspapers reported a small attendance at his funeral. Under the title "Irish Writer Praised by Dorothy Parker", *The Daily Telegraph* (3 February 1997) talks about his time at The Gate Theatre. The familiar facts are given: that he was born in 1920, son of a wheelwright; that he left school at eight years old, and made his first link with writing by auditioning with MacLiammóir and Edwards when he was 16, then proceeding to work in wardrobe at The Gate Theatre. The obituary goes on to recount his success in the US and Britain with his novels, in particular *The Countrywoman*, and tells a curious tale about a moment of breakdown. "But Smith did not prosper. In 1967 he had been involved in a bankruptcy suit brought by Irene Handl, who claimed to have lent him £9800 in Melbourne. Smith, who had been undergoing psychiatric treatment, revealed that his assets amounted to the 18s 2d in his pockets, while his debts added up to £11,232." It concludes with the summing up, "Paul Smith had none of the easy amiability conventionally ascribed to the Irish; rather like Swift, he was one whose breast was lacerated by savage indignation." I can't say that accords with my brief encounter with him. Rather, I would have to say that I found him courteous and above all honest, if a little wary and cautious. *The Irish Times* continued, "Smith was ever the outsider, and his honesty remained his defining quality both as a writer and as an individual." It ends with the terse comment that "Paul Smith never married." Was this a euphemistic way of saying that he was gay? I assume so, and I have always assumed that he was, for a number of reasons. Partly because of his connection with MacLiammóir and Edwards, partly because of his powerful writing around same-sex desire, partly because of the reference to the American post-graduate student (two of his books are dedicated with love to Allen, a very daring dedication for a male writer in the 1960s), and mainly because of the warmth of his friendship with Kate O'Brien. In a sense, if he was gay, then this must have been an important and empowering part of his journey from tenement to bohemia, the transcending of class enabled by a common sexual identity. For the gay men MacLiammóir and Edwards and the lesbian Kate O'Brien, this common ground would have created a link with the young Paul Smith, and aided him on his path towards creative expression – and Smith was always clear to acknowledge the importance of this for him. The entry on Smith in the new *Dictionary of Irish Biography*, published in 2009, verifies much of his biographical detail, including the fact that his father, a violent and alcoholic man, had served in the British Army during the First World War; and so confirms that *The Countrywoman* drew on autobiographical sources. It includes the information that Smith worked with Orson Welles as a costume designer, unaccredited, on the film version of *Othello* in 1952 (very possible given Smith's links with The Gate Theatre and the fact that he moved back to Ireland in 1972), was made a member of Aosdána and was given the American Irish Foundation Literary Award in 1978. It also gives what must be judged a fair assessment of Smith's overall career: "While details of his autobiography supplied by Smith to publishers and interviewers must be evaluated with caution, when speaking of writing or the inner truth of his experience, he was fearlessly honest. His work is remarkably uneven, often within a single book, segments of which may be ill-conceived, unconvincing or bombastic. Always a compelling writer, he composed numerous good passages and one great book." I assume that *The Countrywoman* is the one great book and it is the book most commonly remembered, even on his memorial tablet.

As I write this, I can look out my window onto the backs of the houses Smith writes about in his novels, the big red-brick houses around Portobello, Leeson Park and Dartmouth Square. Someone, maybe someone homeless, has started a fire in the lane outside my window on this cold January afternoon. Smith described this exact lane in one passage in *Summer Sang in Me*: "On Northbrook Road leaves falling from trees lay idle and curled, desolate on shorn lawns ... Behind the houses on one side of the road, the lane into which we had drifted stretched from Ranelagh at one end to Leeson Park and the church the Protestant had lifted at the other. In the lane, girls in caches of clothes gone gray from too much washing stood tethered to fellas who smoothered with their mouths the girls' whimpers of ruin." From where I sit writing this, in five minutes, I can walk to the bridge on the Grand Canal by Charlemont Street and read that memorial tablet:

Earth does not understand her child
Who from the loud, gregarious town
Returns, depleted and defiled,
To the still woods, to fling him down.
Earth cannot count the sons she bore:
The wounded lynx, the wounded man
Come trailing blood unto her door;
She shelters both as best she can.

He must have asked to be remembered in this way himself and I presume he chose these lines of poetry himself, given his fondness for the poetry of Edna St Vincent Millay. He even used the title "Come Trailing Blood" for an adaptation of his first novel, *Esther's Altar*. Why this poem, called "The Return"? Was he himself the wounded lynx, the wounded man, returning to his point of origin, seeking shelter? So much of his fiction is about the wounded women and children of the tenements, all doomed to death or entrapment in squalor; but Paul Smith himself escaped, remade himself and went on to live a life of creative fulfilment and success. What interests me most was that after all that travel he wanted to return and to be remembered at the place where he began, the source of his two best novels, *the loud gregarious town*. I should have taken the time to read his novels and I could have asked him something about his life; but at least I had the sense to realize that valuable opportunity Lorna Reynolds was offering me, and made my way to Blackrock to meet Paul Smith over 20 years ago. His novels deserve to survive.

*Born in Waterford in 1962, Eibhear Walshe was educated at De La Salle College and University College Dublin. He is the author of three books: a biography (*Kate O'Brien: A Writing Life, *Irish Academic Press, 2006), a memoir (*Cissie's Abattoir, *The Collins Press, 2009), and a critical study (*Oscar's Shadow: Wilde, Homosexuality and Modern Ireland, *Cork University Press, 2012). He is a Senior Lecturer in the School of Modern English, University College, Cork.*

OUT AND ABOUT

—

David Kinloch

In Glasgow and New York.

from GAFF

1

In the middle of the sky above the woods
a peregrine prepares to stoop
on songbird or small waterfowl,

loses its straight path down
through layers of air and spray,
its nictitating eyelids blinking

in the sudden gleam that jumps out
from the bling of bracelets on Stu's
wrist. Even at this altitude

it can make out the mouse-soft fuzz
that has escaped his shave, his eyes
– those delicacies – his claws

which thrust the undergrowth
aside. Stu is too big to kill
but no frustration shivers

through the peregrine
which slows feet first
into its bald tree above the falls.

2

Stu'd prepped this evening cruise
with customary skill, browsed
all the on-line drag-queen stores

and had a treasure chest of out-fits
at his tips; Clyde Falls was Nature
at the best of times: mud with water

the underpainting's pigment. Sturdy
hurdies needed tweeds and woollens
but girded by the booty boosters

only Stu knew how to model.
In Janet's Closet he'd basketed
the ultimate pink hiding gaff,

a waist nipper with garter straps
and a two-hook bra extender pack.
Dizzy with the brewage of his spoils,

(anticipation more than half the fun)
he'd gazed at camisoles and pencil skirts,
plumping for a wench top and a giraffe

long sleeve blouse to dapple up
his ample lap in case Summer came along.
Square-heel Maryjanes would suit the paths

by Corra Linn if it was dry and thigh-high
leather boots if damp. He'd spent an age
selecting a good eye explosives kit

but soon he'd painted on a country realness
that made him fierce and winsome.
He looked a picture in his compact glass

lip-syncing for his life, ready Girl,
to break the dawn, to meet the soul m8
in the Folly, above the gorge, among the woods.

3

Falcon flows transverse
to the strike of the Silurian
strata through streams of upper air.

He knows the watershed, the drainage
country and the toil of long dark
gorges where he'll perch but never fish.

The flat haughs of the Clyde
are little squares that grow
to fit his eyes then swallow

him completely before his claws
pull up a starling, swift or vole
and he swings strongly

to the moor or back up
to the maws of hungry young.
Hovering above the Linns

he waits for food to twist
the undergrowth, the paths
beside the trough, knows

how all turns and dies
if it breaks cover,
if he can look at them.

4

Stu is out now in the twilight. He's parked
his car by Lanark Mill, noted number plates
of fellow travelers: Miss Mafia

is somewhere up ahead and Meryl
Streep. Each has their favourite
beat. Stu is queen of the pavilion,

a ruined folly over famous falls
from which a Princess leapt
and drowned. The glamour

of it suits him well although
he keeps a knightly cosh
beneath his tweeds

for summer keelies up from town
stuck on glue and prejudice.
Stu passes by the hide

where Jack and Mick keep friendly
eyes on peregrines: they smile
and share a fag. And then the "rerr burd!"

sashays on, the chafe of stockings
lost among the chase of waters.
The mirk gets murkier,

a smirr of rain laces Stu's new lashes,
a rabbit dashes out and into bushes,
his heels get stuck in duckboard cracks.

Stu curses, twists, looks up
to see the falcon – still – above him,
wonders, yanks out his foot

and passes on. About the Water
Board's big pipe he turns and climbs
towards the summerhouse,

ignoring viewpoints from the lower
terraces, his calves now straining
at the woollen tights. Higher

loom the ruined stones, smart
lintels, empty windows and the balustrade
from which who knows

once looked, admired or – back
to vantage point – hatched a Claude Mirror
on the scene, catching out a corner of the Falls

beyond her shoulder and taming them
to a mellow picturesque.
Now he settles to his smoke

and waits, its wisp just visible
to those who care to look.
Some nights that's all he does:

just smokes and waits,
waits among the fag ends, the droppings,
thistle-stalks and docken leaves,

propped against the door frame,
feet planted on the pockmarked
steps. Most rustlings he ignores,

past mistress of the different
prints small creatures make
upon the evening air.

And often he's imagined up
past denizens: laughter barked
across the upper storey,

the steam and sweat
of kitchen lads where he now leans.
But most of all the ladies:

bustle, hoop and taffeta,
tea taken, the scent of powder,
snuff.

A man in jeans or leather
suddenly across the folly's floor
stops the dream. Stu unlaces,

and all the tension of the climb,
the wait, goes up in pleasure
as the folly fits its purpose once again.

5

Falcon tholes the blanket of wet
air that covers him at nest.
All seems to be inverted:

beneath are clouds of mist,
above the fall of water;
nothing but the pat, pit, pat

of leaves, cobwebs now
a tangled streak of grey.
He squats gently on his young

pushing them to sleep
among the fibrous mass
of feathers, tucks in

his own slim head and waits.
First will come the storm sway:
his eyes lit up by scraps of day

will plunge through bright and dark
although they're shut up
fast against the Linn's

expanding roar. He waits.
He knows the calm will come
and with it dove and magpie,

pigeon, mouse and blackbird,
small raptors and the unwise
gulls heading back to sea.

6

"Fuck", Stu thinks, and touches
the Farrah Fawcett ringlets
uncurling round his face;

The "Cybil" or "Shania"
were made for stormy weather
no sun up in the sky

but Farrah is his lucky
face which soon begins to run.
"Fuck fuck fuck fuck"

Stu thinks, and then of Meryl
and Miss Mafia back now
in their cars no doubt with flasks

of hot tomato soup. His beau'd
been worth it though: a plucky
little college stud down

to work his parents' pub;
polite, a ladies man in fact
who knew the nooks and crannies

of the Linns. He'd scarpered
when the first zigzag
had cleaved them both apart

leaving Stu to damp apparel.
"If only the folly's mirrors
were still here", he reflected,

"spanking pier glasses, Lady
Shallot's full length shot,
big fuckers I could use

to get my gear together".
Stu moved to the centre
of the folly and held

his compact up, his face
— moon-small — shining down
at him from powdered rims.

Was it the brew of fractured
light and rain strewn
across the glass, his flesh,

that put her there — as
suddenly as the boy had come —
this ghostly girl with young

man's face drowning under
— was it rain or the waterfall
itself becoming her: Corra

Linn that leapt like lightning
across the chasm
of the compact mirror?

Stu started back in fear.
Was this him, this fearsome
girl, disheveled, sinking

then surging up to him
again, an arm outstretched
– a branch, a bat wing

lit for seconds as it
sounded out the Folly's
limits – his sister

pursued eternally
to that uncanny fall
into the deep, wet

depths of her identity?
Stu staggered, turned
towards the empty window frames

that moved now, grew
silver skins of light-lit
rain and recomposed themselves

as mirrors. And there Stu saw
with horror all the Linns
of Clyde pour from the rocky

lintels of the Folly, all
the waters: Elvan, Glengonner,
Garf and Midlock Water,

Camps, Little Clyde's Burn,
all with his terror in their sights.
The folly filled with folly

as he flailed about like salmon
leaping from an element
that was his and not his.

Stu swam towards the entrance
and gained the steps;
there – panting, shivering –

he looked up to find
a wooden door that dammed
the flood against him

and as he gingerly pulled
down his sodden skirt
around his knees

discovered two peepholes
shadowed by the faint
imprint of many faces.

Stu didn't hesitate
and clamped his eyes
to holes that fitted perfectly.

At first his gaze crossed over
a river's black abyss and then
dead centre through the chink

he spied three ladies dressed
for Summer laughing up
at mirrors from which the Falls

cascaded down on parasols
above their heads. Dry
as bones, they twirled

about like whirligigs
till only one was left.
This girl then turned

towards a painting
of the Falls and as she
turned the whole frame

cracked from side to side
and again the waters poured
tearing at her clothes,

her hair. She clung hard
to the flimsy parasol
and through the birl

of its kaleidoscopic
whirl, Stu saw it morph,
become a gas-fueled lamp,

its blue flame illuminating
every crevice of the peephole's gaff.

With a cry Stu thrust
the doors aside, ready
for the river's rush,

ready to swim the circling
dark to save the girl,
to sacrifice himself

which somehow seemed
a saving too. He stopped.
No flood floored him.

No corpse bobbed
against the roofless folly.
There was a tunnel,

tar black, and when he stepped
out of the pinhole at the very
end everything was mild

and dry and gauzy as if he stood
within an illustration, some parts
of which seemed half alive

and others still and lifeless.
The girl lay naked on a bank
of twigs and hedgerow flowers;

her legs akimbo, the sex
a mirror of the gash
from which the background

waterfall gleamed but did not
spill. Stu knelt and touched
her ice-cold skin, jumped

back: for it was parchment,
leather, yet her arm which held
the lamp was warm and moving

slightly. Stu could not see her face.
And though he tried, he could not push
the black tunnel's edge aside

to find her head. Stu knelt
within the crook her arm described
and wept and smiled: he'd never made it

to the wooden doorway,
had dallied among parasols,
but even in this dream … look!

he could not wholly drown,
must kneel beside, not be,
this scattering of limbs

which still held up a little
light as if to toast the Falls,
ignite them, make them real.

Stu wiped the tears away,
took out his compact glass
to check the smoky eyes

and there, the wing-tip
of a falcon brushed
his face and he cried out

with the raptor's fierce,
hermetic voice and closed
the peephole with his claws.

7

Falcon woke the moment the Falls
changed their key and light
began to climb the tree.

Carefully, he stretched his wings
and beat the air then launched,
keeping to the snaking flight path

of the spate; and there, he saw
a thing with eyes corralled
by waters frothing in from every side,

floating in the middle of the dark
sleek pool. It seemed cocooned
by river weeds

but as the falcon glanced
away and soared he heard
the first notes of a song

no songbird ever made
and beat higher, desperate
to escape its lure.

MEMORY

after Rimbaud and Arthur Rimbaud in New York *by David Wojnarowicz*

I Under Brooklyn Bridge

Brackish; like the sour nickel tang of that first blow job;
the assault on the stanchions' darkness by the shadows of men's bodies;
gleaming mail, silk sleeves of skin that tack and yaw,
brandished beneath the bridge they give their motion to.

a flurry of furies – No ... the viscous piss arcs
slowly, tributaries among the estuary of puddles. He
goes down in the canopied dusk, drawing in
the others' dimness and the arch.

II In New York's Subway

Ah! the subway's rotted windows reflect its murky broth!
A strip light fillets the recumbent bodies, prepped and floating.
A girl's green legs are crossed and recrossed
against the urgent need to go.

A clown on the seat opposite winks his yellow eyelid,
mimicking the baw faced mask that stares at him
– *je est un autre* – O Obi Wan!
Next, it's London; or the thick grey heat of Charleville.

III As Duchamp

"The silence of Marcel Duchamp" – a right little madam –
"is overrated"; spraycanned on the john's wall, it is even
disproportionate next to the graffiti of Vitruvian man
taken from behind; kids drop acid on the tarmacadam

just out of shot. Oh, he'll tuck up his arms again
and take off for Switzerland, Ethiopia or *Alex*
in Wonderland where the froth aye overflows
the rim; take after himself taking off.

IV At West Side Pier with Graffiti

Grass was a joy; pure and simple; but the big
sketched-in syringe and your whole dwarfed body
tells you to go now and ferret out the scag, tap
the last mainline into the piers' spare arms.

The acoustic for tears is pitch perfect down here.
Traffic doesn't penetrate; you can hear a rat shit.
After, when you surface into the grey, unanchored
surface there's one old guy cruising you, breathing heavily.

V *Target Practice*

I can't shoot straight but my long, bound arm
always hits the target: the bull's eye is child's play
and I push my boat right out of its concentric
circles until the world becomes a large blue marigold.

My chains catch on its teeth and pull them out;
my head, pinned to the wall, floats free,
punctured but unbowed. I set sail:
legless, just a ring, a ring of roses.

Author's Note: "Memory" is an experiment in ekphrasis as translation — and vice-versa. It is written with one eye on the images and form of Arthur Rimbaud's poem "Mémoire", sometimes classed among the "Derniers vers", and another eye on a series of photographs by the American artist David Wojnarowicz. This series is entitled "Rimbaud in New York" and offers shots of the photographer himself and some of his friends posing in various New York locations wearing face masks made from a famous photograph of the French poet.

David Kinloch was born in 1959, and raised and educated in Glasgow. He is a graduate of the universities of Glasgow and Oxford and was for many years a teacher of French Studies. A founder editor of the poetry journal Verse, *he is the author of five collections of poems, most recently* Finger of a Frenchman *(Carcanet, 2011). He currently teaches Creative Writing and Scottish Literature at the University of Strathclyde, Glasgow.*

REQUIEM FOR THE *TITANIC*

The following suite of brief essays, literary reflections and quotations was first published in the programme for the composer Philip Hammond's major musical composition, Requiem for the Lost Souls of the Titanic *(for Mezzo-soprano, Chorus and Brass). The performance took place on the evening of 14 April 2012 — the centenary of the sinking of the* Titanic — *before an audience of nearly 1,000 at St Anne's Cathedral, Belfast. Glenn Patterson's literary reflections were incorporated within the musical composition. The programme was commissioned by Belfast Titanic Company, and was edited and produced by* Irish Pages. *Philip Hammond (b. 1951) is one of Ireland's foremost composers.*

A TERRIBLE SILENCE

Michael McCaughan

Glittering in the dark.

It is Sunday morning, 14 April 1912, and *Titanic* is more than halfway across the Atlantic on her maiden voyage to New York. Under the command of Captain E.J. Smith, the pride of the White Star Line is westbound with around 2,200 souls on board, but only enough lifeboats for 1,178.

Titanic's marine splendour is the embodiment of the Edwardian age at sea. She reflects the social fabric and self-confidence of the era, enshrining faith in technology and progress. Built in Belfast at the leading edge of shipbuilding skill, *Titanic* incorporates advanced safety features. In the event of an accident, watertight doors can be closed electronically, making the ship "practically unsinkable". *Titanic* is intended to be her own lifeboat in an emergency. White Star advertising assures passengers that "the time given to slumber and rest will be free of noise or other disturbance".

However, if *Titanic* is the essence of modernity and engineering achievement, she is also invested with misplaced certainties and reckless complacency about the number of lifeboats carried. As the great liner steams on, all are oblivious to the iceberg ahead and the imminence of destruction and death.

During the day, *Titanic* picks up wireless messages from other ships reporting the presence of ice. At 9.40 p.m., a report comes in giving the position of icebergs across *Titanic*'s course, but it is not delivered to the bridge. Nevertheless, by the evening of 14 April, Captain Smith and his officers know that *Titanic* is entering a region where ice can be expected. Despite this, *Titanic*'s speed is not reduced.

At 11.40 p.m., look-outs in the crow's nest report an iceberg ahead. The officer of the watch, Mr Murdoch, immediately turns the ship hard to port, reverses the engines and closes the watertight doors. Still travelling at over 20 knots, *Titanic* scrapes past the iceberg on the starboard side. A head-on collision is averted but *Titanic* is mortally damaged by an underwater spur of ice tearing at her hull in grinding impact. In less than 10 seconds, *Titanic* is pierced below the waterline for a length of 300 feet. The pumps cannot cope with the huge inrush of water flooding into the five forward compartments.

Thomas Andrews, Harland & Wolff's Chief Designer, quickly realizes that *Titanic* cannot survive such massive and unforeseen damage. She has been designed to float with any two of her sixteen compartments flooded, but with five compartments rapidly filling, the ship is doomed. Inevitably the great liner will sink by the bows as water flows from compartment to compartment over the top of the bulkheads. Andrews calculates that *Titanic* has about two hours to live.

At 12.05 a.m., preparations to launch the lifeboats begin. Stewards start rousing passengers, helping with lifejackets and getting them to the boat deck.

At 12.15 a.m., the first wireless distress signals are transmitted. *Titanic*'s plight is widely picked up but ships cannot reach her in time. *Titanic*'s signals continue until 2.17 a.m., when they end abruptly.

From 12.15 a.m. until 1.45 a.m., distress-signal rockets are fired from the boat deck, but there is no response.

About 12.20 a.m., lifeboats are swung out from the boat deck, followed by the order: "women and children first". By 12.45 a.m., the boats are being lowered but not all are filled to capacity. Some women are frightened of the 65-foot descent; others refuse to abandon their husbands. There is reluctance to leave the supposed safety of the ship. Third-class passengers are at a disadvantage, as they can only reach the boat deck through the first- and second-class accommodation. As lifeboats are being lowered, many men are standing back, but others take available spaces, including J. Bruce Ismay, Chairman of White Star.

By 1.50 a.m., the last of the lifeboats are leaving and fear and panic are palpable in the mass of people left behind.

For many, the watchwords of the night are duty, self-sacrifice and stoicism in the face of death. The two wireless operators tap out signals to the last. One survives; the other is lost. The engineers, deep in the ship, remain at their posts to maintain electrical power and keep the lights burning. All are lost. Thomas Andrews is also lost, his chief concern the safety of everyone but himself. On the boat deck, eight musicians of the ship's orchestra play ragtime tunes to keep passengers' spirits up as the disaster unfolds. Near the end, bandmaster Wallace Hartley chooses the hymn "Nearer, My God, to Thee" as their final piece and epitaph.

Titanic's decks are now steeply tilting as her bow sinks deeper and her stern rises higher out of the water. All the boats have gone. Hundreds and hundreds of people, hanging on to life, are crowding aft on the upending ship, still glittering in the darkness.

It is after 2.00 a.m. and *Titanic* is sinking fast. About 2.15 a.m., the sea engulfs the bridge, where Captain Smith is alone at his post. At 2.20 a.m., *Titanic* plunges to the deep. As the ship goes down, hundreds are entombed in her hull and hundreds more are in the water, drowning and freezing to death. From the safety of lifeboats, the living hear the awful cries of the dying. Then a terrible silence, life extinguished.

Fifteen hundred souls are lost. How can this be? How can it be imagined? How can it be told?

Michael McCaughan is an Irish maritime historian living in Belfast. He is the author of The Birth of the Titanic *(Blackstaff Press, 1998), and was a curator at the Ulster Folk and Transport Museum for four decades.*

A PACKED LAUNCH

Keith Haines

A deferential age.

RMS *Titanic* was rescued from nearly half a century of embarrassment and obscurity by Belfast-born film-maker William MacQuitty, a witness to the vessel's launch, in *A Night to Remember* (1958). The memory of *Titanic* had been submerged even before the Great War. Ballymacarrett homes may have preserved relics of the liner smuggled from the yard – carpentry veneers, carpet offcuts – but its achievement was even then silting over on the ocean bed.

Survival on *Titanic* was partly dependent upon social status, and the railway line that bisected East Belfast at Holywood Arches – with industrial Ballymacarrett to the west and residential Sydenham and Belmont to the east – manifested a fault-line in the class-ridden society that built the vessel. Workmanship in Harland & Wolff (H&W), as in all the industries of East Belfast – despite all the wealth generated – was poorly compensated. This was reflected in the scene, as *Titanic* glided down the slipway, of workmen racing to harvest the tallow that lubricated the incline. It was a contradiction that entrepreneurs such as Gustav Wolff, who also founded the adjacent Belfast Ropework Company and created thousands of jobs, felt obliged to donate large sums to local charities. Wolff resided on the Sydenham side of the Arches divide; his patronizing doggerel, "But give me my house, though it may be a garret, / In the pleasant surroundings of Ballymacarrett", owed more to rhyme than to geographical reason.

East Belfast industrialists were creative pioneers as well as capable businessmen; one memorial said of Harland (1895): "he is entitled to take his place amongst the great inventors of the last half of the century". Thomas Andrews, who designed (and died on) *Titanic*, was a popular employer and a talented shipbuilder, but tributes could prove retrospectively ironic; when working on *Oceanic* (1899), then the largest ship in the world, one poet had lauded his skills: "May your hand ne'er lose its cunning, we don't care how winds may roar, / For we know we have a frigate that can sail from shore to shore". These men were lionized in life and apotheosized in death; the *Belfast News-Letter* penned unctuously and unjustifiably about William Pirrie that he deserved "to be singled out as one of the most notable industrial pioneers who have ever made their mark in history".

Pirrie ruled H&W imperiously, without compunction, dispensing with those who no longer served his aspirations and, in the Roman imperial style, treated the launch of *Titanic* as "bread and circuses". The thronged occasion on 31 May 1911, like the ship itself, was carefully engineered – partly to coincide with the joint birthdays of Lord and Lady Pirrie. It was conducted in haste and received less fanfare than had the launch of its sister ship, *Olympic*, seven months earlier. *Titanic* was in a less advanced state of readiness than had been *Olympic* (and indeed *Oceanic*) at the time of her launch, and it took three months longer to make her operational. That day was also a singular opportunity to display the sister ships afloat in tandem, as *Olympic* (which had been popularly opened for public inspection four days previously) was launched at 2.00 p.m. on the same day from the newly constructed largest graving dock in the world.

Pirrie may also have hoped that plaudits would create a distraction from the intensifying political crisis in Belfast – in which his own role was becoming more suspect. The Chairman had opposed Home Rule in its earlier manifestations, but now alienated much of his workforce – already infected with dangerous notions of socialism and trade unionism – with his more sympathetic utterances, designed to lubricate his personal ingratiation into London society. It was another noted Home Ruler, Rev J.B. Armour of Ballymoney, who wrote, 10 days after the tragedy: "I hear the *Titanic* disaster holds public attention still, as it has been overwhelmingly awesome and made the stoutest hold his breath for some time."

Such sentiments were, however, unwelcome to Pirrie and he worked hard to dampen the memory of the catastrophe. Despite the fact that in Thomas Andrews he had not only lost a managing director but also a nephew, Pirrie closed the yard for only one day as a tribute to those local people who had drowned. As the history of the shipyard reveals, he ensured that, at the Mersey Inquiry, "H&W were exonerated and the quality of workmanship praised". In a deferential age, Pirrie manipulated the local press to keep adverse coverage to a minimum. On the first anniversary, there was a mere half a column in memory of the tragedy; a further year later, any reference had been completely submerged by paramilitary developments in Ulster. Ironically, the *Belfast Evening Telegraph*, owned by W&G Baird (of which William MacQuitty's father had been Managing Director), appears to have given no acknowledgement to either pre-war anniversary.

The sensitivity of H&W prevailed for half a century, culminating in a refusal to allow access to the yard to shoot any footage of *A Night to Remember*. *Titanic* had by the mid-1950s become a neglected misadventure. There had been no concerted outcry in 1935 against the dismantling of the surviving link to its memory, *Olympic*. The revival of interest in *Titanic* dates from the determination of William MacQuitty to reconstruct the tragedy on film. On becoming a nonagenarian, MacQuitty committed his accumulated experience and reflection to print in *Survival Kit*, wherein he offers this criticism of early twentieth-century educational philosophy: it did not recognize "that ambitions for security and indispensability are delusions, that the winners are likely to become the richest men in the cemetery". It is an appropriate, eloquent epitaph for *Titanic*.

Keith Haines is a local historian living in Belfast. He is the author of Images of East Belfast *(The History Press, 2007).*

REMEMBER THE SUBMERGED

John Wilson Foster

A transcendent calamity.

Even before the rescue ship *Carpathia* arrived in New York with survivors, *Titanic* had become the "ill-fated" liner. The journalistic epithet persevered, because it seemed fitting to see some invisible hand at work in the sinking. The disaster was so monumental, and after *Carpathia* docked, so undeniable, that it seemed uncannily ordained once shock wore off. W.T. Stead, the most famous casualty, had predicted for years a maritime accident with enormous fatalities, but it was more than real-world probability. A handful of poets and storywriters had commended predictions to paper of startling and disconcerting detail. The poet Thomas Hardy saw the ship caught in cosmic crossfire: "No mortal eye could see / The intimate welding of their later history", he wrote of the growing ship and iceberg. Was it a more credulous time? Young Edith Evans refused to be rescued because she had been told by a London fortune-teller that she would meet her death on the water; she left the lifeboat before it was launched and perished. Her ghost appears in T.S. Eliot's poem, *The Waste Land*, in its potent line, "Fear death by water".

Yet without any such superstition, we can still be appalled by a calamity that seems like some mammoth force at our unprotected backs. We might even see *Titanic* as the only ship that is seeking us, like the ship in Philip Larkin's poem, "towing at her back / A huge and birdless silence". In short, we are still afraid, for we are all passengers on *Titanic*.

In hindsight, it was some species of fate. At the time, on board, so much was chance and mischance. Some saved, some condemned, on a vagary. Suddenly those on board were enacting "the state of manne, and how he is called at uncertayne tymes by death, and when he thinketh least thereon".

After all, around the lifeboats there was the appearance of a holiday crowd – some in casual dress, some in covered pyjamas, some in evening dress. J. Bruce Ismay wore carpet slippers while he shepherded passengers into the lifeboats. But the writer Helen Churchill Candee, who survived, later likened the scene to "a fancy-dress ball in Dante's Hell".

When the last lifeboats left, perspective was everything. Some of those in the boats had leisure to acknowledge the starry moonless night. W.B. Yeats left no poetry of the disaster, but his famous phrase was anticipated by a survivor who wrote of the "terrible beauty" of *Titanic*, electric lights blazing in every cabin and on every deck, as she sank head down. But though it is painful, we must remember those left on board when the last boat left, abandoned to their own frail devices. As the sinking proceeded, the familiar options, potential and variety of their lives dwindled. The company would have become less reassuring and at last comfortless. A survivor saw the sinking ship as a swarming beehive, "but the bees were men" clinging to the stern or leaping into the ocean.

Archibald Gracie was one of those who decided to abandon ship just before she abandoned him, and he saved himself by a heroic underwater swim. He heard from the human debris field created when the ship vanished "the agonizing cries of death from over a thousand throats, the wails and groans of the suffering … ": it is difficult to read on. One survivor wrote, "the horror, the helpless horror", echoing the famous words from Conrad's *Heart of Darkness*.

But others, those with a code of behaviour to follow, turned away from the panic and quietly faced death. We seize on inspiring stories of heroic composure and stories of conduct beyond the call of duty (Jack Phillips in the Marconi shack, the Guarantee Group from Harland & Wolff), to allay the horror of what happened when the ship forsook its passengers. Our still point of this overturning world must be the much-loved Thomas Andrews, last seen by survivors lost in thought before Norman Wilkinson's painting, *Approach to Plymouth Harbour*, in the first-class smoking-room, far from the maddened crowd.

Joseph Conrad denounced the "false, written-up, Drury Lane aspects" of the disaster, but the maiden voyage was a quasi-theatrical event with an extraordinary decor and cast of players. The sinking occupied in time a staged Shakespearian drama. One woman survivor recalled that "it all seemed like a play that was being enacted for entertainment". Two French survivors thought that from their lifeboat *Titanic* was "like some fantastic piece of stage scenery".

It is often merely theatrical spectacle that draws us now, and understandably, but at the time it was also the morality the disaster seemed to depict. The playwright Henry Arthur Jones was among those who met *Carpathia* in New York and he called the sinking "a transcendent calamity". The disembarking survivors he describes are like a troop of exhausted players, all with stories, and composing the human procession. The disaster still retains the power of *Everyman* or the *Divine Comedy*. Peruse the list of the lost and you might think in grim surprise of Eliot's line from Dante: "I had not thought death had undone so many".

And they are whom we must keep in mind. It may not be difficult to do so. Some of us relive in the last hours of *Titanic* our primal fears — of darkness, of ice, of falling. It was Virginia Woolf's fascination with drowning that drew her to the *Titanic* inquiry and led her to weave the disaster into her first novel. We might also relive our fear of precipices and chasms. We are haunted by those still on the ship, borne under the waves, departing on that voyage to the Sohm Abyssal Plain. We recall E.M. Forster's admonition in *Howards End*: "remember the submerged".

John Wilson Foster was born and raised in Belfast, educated in Eugene, Oregon, taught in Vancouver, British Columbia and now lives in Portaferry, Co Down. He is a freelance writer and literary critic and an honorary research fellow at Queen's University Belfast. He has published three books on RMS Titanic and twelve other books on Irish, English and American literature, natural history, and Irish culture. He has been a folksinger and songwriter. A lifelong birder, he has studied and enjoyed the birds of the Fraser River delta near where he lived in Vancouver, and of Strangford Lough where he now lives.

———

REMEMBRANCE
———

Michael Longley

Hail and pebbles.

In recent months I have visited the First World War battlefields and cemeteries of the Somme Valley in Northern France; and, in Berlin, the Memorial to the

Murdered Jews of Europe. In both instances the memorialists' dilemma has been how to approach atrociousness; how to make room in our imaginations for enormity. In France, guided by the genius of Edwin Lutyens, the Commonwealth War Graves Commission opted for the same simple headstone for all ranks. The hundreds of thousands of graves are arranged in rows that conjure pattern out of chaos and create a monument to emptiness and sorrow. To Lutyens we owe the profound concept of the cenotaph (the empty tomb) and the tomb of the unknown warrior, as well as the overwhelmingly sorrowful Thiepval Memorial to the 72,194 missing of the Somme, the dead soldiers whose bodies were never found. Clean abstract imagery clears the way for our mourning. At the entrance to each cemetery there's a register of all the soldiers buried there, and a visitors' book. Each of us remembers someone (in my case, my father, who joined up as a boy soldier in the London Scottish in 1914); or we read the personal messages previous visitors have left behind to be shared between us and the ghosts: "The lads did well", "We came to remember", "Remembering Uncle Bob".

The Ulster Memorial near the hamlet of Thiepval replicates Helen's Tower at Clandeboye, where the Ulster Division trained before going to fight in France. It would have been one of the last meaningful Irish landmarks that the young soldiers would have seen before leaving for the trenches. The Ulster Tower helps us to remember what they remembered.

In Berlin the Memorial to the Murdered Jews of Europe consists of hundreds of rows of concrete slabs or stelae that are low as you enter and then get increasingly taller as you proceed towards the centre of the vast site. It was minus 15 degrees when I was there. Each great black slab was covered in hailstones. I was reminded of the Jewish custom of placing a pebble on a headstone. The memorial slabs stretched out of sight down each sub-zero corridor, and I wondered if there would be enough hailstones to represent the murdered millions. I thought of my friend the late Helen Lewis, who survived Auschwitz, and of Paul, her first husband, who perished there. I pictured the terrible numbers tattooed on Helen's arm. This great memorial seemed capable of refracting in the snow-light such fragilities and at the same time providing in the centre of a major city a silence adequate for the vastness of our lamentation.

When contemplating death it seems helpful to walk among standing stones, to incorporate their stillness with our momentum. The memorial stones become part of our lives, their patterns part of the farmland of Northern France (death's crop) or, in Berlin, a sort of compacted suburb.

The Memorial to the Murdered Jews of Europe and Edwin Lutyens' designs are great works of art, art that conceals art. The schmaltzy Titanic Memorial in the grounds of Belfast's City Hall shows how difficult it is to hit the right note. It tries too hard and looks as though it has been sculpted out of toilet soap. The wreck of the great liner lies on the ocean floor with fish swimming in and out of her portholes. Our imaginations are inundated with watery images. With its abstract precisions and limitless suggestiveness, music is probably the best way to convey the weirdness of this tragedy. We are blessed to have in Philip Hammond a splendid Irish composer who will listen to the sea and bring back to us the voices of the drowned.

Michael Longley was the holder of the Ireland Chair of Poetry between 2007 and 2010. The rotating three-year chair was established by the Arts Councils in Ireland, Trinity College Dublin, Queen's University Belfast, and University College Dublin to recognize the exceptional achievement of Irish poets in world literature. He is the author of 13 collections of poetry, most recently A Hundred Doors *(Cape, 2011). He continues to live in Belfast.*

GHOSTLY AND AMBIGUOUS

Patricia Craig

Undercurrent.

Belfast's relationship with the *Titanic* has always been complicated. It includes a mixture of chagrin and celebration, along with a wish to commemorate the *Titanic* dead. Enormous pride surrounded the building and launching of the famous ship in the shipyard of Harland & Wolff in the opening years of the twentieth century. And Belfast exultation in the great achievement, the stupendous feat of shipbuilding, outlasted the *Titanic*'s loss. But after the disaster the city's pride was tempered by a certain wryness. The "practically unsinkable" had, after all, sunk. It had not survived its encounter with a hazard of the natural world in the form of the iceberg. So much for hubris and over-confidence and braggadocio.

Nevertheless, the *Titanic*'s magnificence and its destiny are tied up together. The effect of the calamity was to make the doomed ship a byword for poignancy. In a sense, it was taken away from its place of origin as it impinged on the world's consciousness. The sheer magnitude of the shipwreck, with the loss of 1,500 lives, created an overwhelming impact. It was swiftly adapted to a variety of symbolic purposes. The *Titanic* became a metaphor for absolutely everything you care to name, from an exploitive capitalist system to an irrecoverable glamour. The ship and its fate made a bridge between two cultural eras, pre- and post-First World War. The catastrophe sounded a warning against materialism and against an aim to outdo the natural order of things (standing in for God). The fall of the *Titanic* was as chastening as that of Lucifer.

As the first shock waves wore off in Belfast, explanations were sought and – because it *was* Belfast – some sectarian assertions came into play. A couple of canards surfaced, as nationalist Belfast, long excluded from the highest shipyard employment, allowed itself a moment of gloating. It was Papish pay-back time. A rumour began to circulate of loyalist workers execrating the pope with every nail hammered in, disturbing the universe and foredooming the ship to a terrible end. Another sinister fragment of lore concerned the *Titanic*'s serial number (was it 39090Z?) and the way it appeared to read "No Pope" when held up to a mirror.

These urban legends were still current in the 1950s, when I was told them by my Catholic grandmother, who took them for gospel truth. Not that I paid much attention. I'd heard of the *Titanic*, just, but it wasn't an aspect of Belfast history I cared to explore. There were times – this was one of them – when the ship and its lethal voyage did not loom large in Belfast iconography, and times when it did. Two revivals of *Titanic* enthusiasm occurred in Belfast, the first sparked off by *A Night to Remember* (1958), which brought the shipwreck with its scope for drama, heroism and *sang-froid* tumbling back into people's minds, and the second, later in the century, following the recovery of the wreckage from the ocean bed. On these occasions (and now, on the hundredth anniversary), it seemed appropriate to reclaim the *Titanic* for Belfast *amour propre* – especially since the bulk of *Titanic* literature was focused on everything about the stricken liner apart from its birthplace. For many international commentators, Belfast's role in the *Titanic* story might as well not have existed.

Belfast people knew better. When I read Louis MacNeice's poem, "Death of an Old Lady", I began to gain an inkling of the strength of *Titanic* mystique as an undercurrent in the life of the city. For the first time, in my mind, the scuppered White Star liner became a symbol for something other than shipyard bigotry. MacNeice's lines about "the wrinkled lough / That had

given a child one shining glimpse / Of a boat so big it was named *Titanic*"
suggested a fairy-tale wonderment, a thing so otherworldly it was bound for
destruction. And it seemed that everyone who was there at the time of the
launching had some remembrance of the occasion engraved on their
consciousness. Before it sailed, the naturalist Edward Allworthy Armstrong
was taken by his father on board the *Titanic*, "the greatest ship that had ever
been built". Maurice Craig's father, like Louis MacNeice, watched the ship
set out on its maiden voyage. And, on 15 April 1912, the family of four-year-
old future poet John Hewitt "heard, incredulous, the news / our safe,
unsinkable *Titanic* burst / ripped by sharp berg while on her maiden cruise"
(as he recalled it in his verse autobiography, *Kites in Spring*).

It's all in the past. The shipyards have gone, the old industries are
defunct, Belfast itself is either reborn as a modern city or utterly destroyed
(depending on your point of view). But the great ship remains — ghostly,
ambiguous — forever sailing out of Belfast Lough, and into a realm of myth.

*A critic, essayist and anthologist, Patricia Craig was born and grew up in Belfast, and lived
for many years in London before returning to Northern Ireland in 1999. She has written
biographies of Elizabeth Bowen and Brian Moore, and edited many anthologies including*
The Oxford Books of Ireland, English Detective Stories, Modern Women's Stories,
The Belfast Anthology *and* The Ulster Anthology. *Her memoir* Asking for Trouble
(Blackstaff Press) was published in 2007. She is a regular contributor to The Irish Times,
The Independent *and the* Times Literary Supplement.

See p. 157 for the launch remarks on Patricia Craig's latest book, A Twisted Root:
Ancestral Entanglements in Ireland *(Blackstaff Press, 2012).*

———

THE REQUIEM'S LITERARY MEDITATIONS
———

Glenn Patterson

To the end of the end.

1

So this is how the end begins ... That first plunge, as stunningly cold as a
face in the basin on a winter's morning, whisking breath away, opening a

door on the boy who stepped out – winter summer spring fall – under the vastness of a Midwest sky along the road to school and all that school would lead him to, *summa cum laude* on *summa cum laude*, commodities, country club, every step then an adventure, every foot fallen now a recapitulation of futures past. I can see it with my eyes shut: the wind making waves in the wheat, the farms small craft flung far and wide, because space like time we had in spades.

Two and a half miles, 13,000 feet: from porch to porch, from surface to seabed, from the beginning to the end of the end.

2

CQD CQD SOS SOS CQD DE MGY MGY
Two of us always two of us
CQD CQD SOS SOS CQD DE MGY MGY
In tandem or rotation
CQD CQD SOS SOS CQD DE MGY MGY
The windowless Marconi Room
CQD CQD SOS SOS CQD DE MGY MGY
Tap-tap-tap tap tap tap
CQD CQD SOS SOS CQD DE MGY MGY
Latitude 41.46 North Longitude 50.14 West
CQD CQD SOS SOS CQD DE MGY MGY
Seek assistance. Immediate assistance
CQD CQD SOS SOS CQD DE MGY MGY
Repeat, repeat assistance
CQD CQD SOS SOS CQD DE MGY MGY
Two of us always two of us
CQD CQD SOS SOS CQD DE MGY MGY
The waterfilled Marconi Room
CQD CQD SOS SOS CQD DE MGY MGY
In the sea, clinging, two of us
CQD CQD SOS SOS CQD DE MGY MGY
And then
CQD CQD SOS SOS CQD DE MGY MGY
Just me
CQD CQD SOS SOS CQD DE MGY MGY

3

Belfast, says J.B. Doyle in his *Tours in Ulster: A Hand-book to the Antiquities and Scenery of the North of Ireland*, published (*With Numerous Illustrations, Chiefly from the Author's Sketch-book*) in 1854 by Hodges and Smith of Grafton Street, booksellers to the university, creates a very different impression on the new arrival than does Dublin, "not only in its general aspect, but in the ordinary deportment of its citizens. The easy, promenading air of the citizens of Dublin contrasts rather unfavourably, in a business point of view, with the active bustling of the Northerns. Here men seem to have something of importance to attend to, and to go about it in right earnest." A bit broad, J.B. Doyle, but not entirely without foundation. Whether it is building things, or tearing them down, bringing harpers from every corner of the kingdom, welcoming a queen with "Erin go Bragh" and "Cead Mille Failte" misspelt in dahlias, or braining one another with cobbles hoked out from the ground beneath our feet, we manifest a singleness of purpose that would scare you. From one week to the next – one day, one hour, one breath – the worst of people and the best.

4

Oh, my honey, oh, my honey, if you could only see me, in my raincoat and my muffler, here on deck, torn between keeping time and trying to keep my feet. Oh, my honey, my honey, honey lamb, if I could only see you to explain, why I couldn't just "jump ship", turn my back on the gig.

The order came to play and we played, but that was twenty minutes from the end of yesterday, and here we are, two hours into today, waltzing and ragging.

Not for Black Brothers, who will bill you, I will stake what's left of my life on it, for damage to the suit.

Not for the White Star Line, who made passengers, second-class, of us, not crew.

Not even any more for those on whom the awful truth is dawning that there will be no other dawn.

We are playing now for one another, brothers of the AMU, for all whom work has thrown together, Liverpool dockers, Rhondda miners, Massachusetts textile workers, for the family of Anna LoPizzo, for roses as well as bread.

Oh, my honey, oh, my honey, if you could only see me, in my raincoat and my muffler here on deck, I like to think you'd blow me a kiss and dance.

5

Because of what we hit we missed the trenches, the Crash, the hungry thirties, the Blitz, the camps, the Bomb. We missed Chaplin, Keaton, *The Birth of a Nation*, we missed Jolson, Garland, *Gone with the Wind*. We missed TV. We missed Dixieland and swing, be-bop, hard bop, we missed Elvis, Little Richard, a wop-bop-a-loo-bop, pompadours and mop tops, and wondering what the world was coming to. We missed birthdays, wedding days, anniversaries, christenings and communions, we missed the other fates we might have met, the deaths we might have died, the influenzas, the cancers, the embolisms, the cirrhoses, the suicides, the simply slipping into sleep. We passed instead into myth, launched a library full of books, enough film to cross the Atlantic three times over, more conspiracy theories than Kennedy, ninety-seven million web-pages, a tourist industry, a requiem or two.

We will live longer than every one of you.

Glenn Patterson was born in 1961 in Belfast and studied on the Creative Writing MA at the University of East Anglia with Malcolm Bradbury. He is the author of eight novels, most recently The Mill for Grinding Old People Young *(Faber, 2012), as well as a collection of literary journalism,* Lapsed Protestant *(New Island, 2006). He is a Lecturer in Creative Writing at Queen's University Belfast.*

———

AN UPENDING WORLD
———

The 9/11 of its day.

"The *Olympic* and *Titanic* are not only the largest vessels in the World; they represent the highest attainments in Naval Architecture and Marine

Engineering; they stand for the pre-eminence of the Anglo-Saxon race on the Ocean ... " (White Star Publicity, 1911)

"All the people on board existed under a sense of false security. How false, it has been sufficiently demonstrated. And the fact which seems undoubted, that some of them actually were reluctant to enter the boats, when told to do so, shows the strength of that falsehood." (Joseph Conrad, *Some Reflections on the Loss of the Titanic*, 1912)

"It is this feeling of irreparable loss which has caused a gloom to settle over the great shipbuilding yard in which *Titanic* had her birth, and neither time nor achievement can dispel the memory of the catastrophe or heal the grief that has taken possession of the hearts of men." (*Belfast News-Letter*, 22 April 1912)

"Many brave things were done that night but none more brave than by those few men playing minute after minute as the ship settled quietly lower and lower in the sea ... the music they played serving alike as their own immortal requiem and their right to be recorded on the rolls of undying fame." (Lawrence Beesley, *Titanic* survivor)

"The sounds of people drowning are something that I can not describe to you, and neither can anyone else. It's the most dreadful sound and there is a terrible silence that follows it." (Eva Hart, *Titanic* survivor)

"Let the Truth be known, no ship is unsinkable. The bigger the ship, the easier it is to sink her. I learned long ago that if you design how a ship'll sink, you can keep her afloat. I proposed all the watertight compartments ... to slow these ships from sinking. In that way, you get everyone off." (Thomas Andrews, Managing Director of Harland & Wolff)

"Our whole civilization is indeed very like the *Titanic*; alike in its power and its impotence, its security and its insecurity..." (G.K. Chesterton, *Illustrated London News*, 1912)

from A DAY WITH EDWARD HOPPER

Derek Coyle

1. The Circle Theatre

You invite us to look in at the woman who
is reading the poster outside the theatre,
the man caught up at the news stand
who wonders what paper to buy.
Then we notice the traffic lights
which seem to look out at us,
those big eyes under the sign
THE CIRCLE THEATRE,
just below the C and E, see,
blocked out by the subway
as it rises out of the ground,
that giant eye worthy of Cyclops
can swallow a multitude in a minute
even now as it absently stares the other way.

2. Pennsylvania Coal Town

His trousers look too short, his waistcoat
a little tight. This bald man hesitates,
stops raking his thin plot of grass
to look up at the light warming
his head, his face, his chest. Shortly,
he will return to his wife and children
via the darkened portico of his house
beside the railroad, not far from the mine
where he earns his living. When he sits
to his supper he'll recall this moment
when he stopped work, and felt
the heat of the retreating sun
and thought this is good.

3. A Woman in the Sun

The sun insists on preaching
its daily sermon, rising high
through your window, its virtues
apparent: steady, independent,

and bright. Some days,
ragged and naked,
you step into its light
to just soak up the heat,

last night's party a memory,
the gin on your breath
an aftertaste, like the high-
heels by the bed, so

you take one long drag
of tobacco and contemplate:
what will it take
to face another Monday?

Derek Coyle was born in Co Kildare in 1971. After undergraduate and postgraduate work in English and Theology at Maynooth, he received his doctorate from the University of Glasgow in 2002. He has published poems and articles in a variety of Irish, British and American publications. He lectures in English Literature and Irish Studies at Carlow College. He currently lives in Carlow.

PORTFOLIO

—

Elizabeth Switaj

Time in the East

West Gate of Angkor Thom, Outside Siem Reap, Cambodia
July 2008

Elizabeth Switaj was born in Seattle in 1980. She holds a BA from the Evergreen State College, an MFA in Poetics and Creative Writing from New College of California, and a PhD in English from Queen's University, Belfast. She taught English for three semesters at Shengda College of Zhengzhou University in China's Henan Province and has travelled throughout East and Southeast Asia.

Her photographs have appeared in a variety of American publications, as well as on the cover of The Nassau Review. *Her first collection of poetry,* Magdalene & the Mermaids, *was published in 2009 by Paper Kite Press, and her pamphlet,* Warburg's Tincture of Sonnets, *is forthcoming from Like This Press. She is the Assistant Managing Editor of this journal.*

Outside Siem Reap, Cambodia
July 2008

Siem Reap, Cambodia
July 2008

Yellow River Scenic Area, Outside Zhengzhou, China
March 2007

Longhu, Zhengzhou, China
March 2007

Red Rock Valley, Yuntai Mountain Geopark, China
September 2007

Beijing, China
September 2007

Terracotta Warriors, Xi'an, China
April 2008

The Great Mosque, Xi'an, China
April 2008

Pudong, Shanghai, China
October 2007

Lake Tonlé Sap, Cambodia
June 2008

Batu Caves, Outside Kuala Lumpur, Malaysia
June 2008

Chinatown, Kuala Lumpur, Malaysia
June 2008

Zhengzhou, China
May 2007

Shengda College, Zhengzhou, China
April 2008

Forbidden City, Beijing, China
December 2007

PORTFOLIO
is generously supported by Nicholson & Bass Ltd, Belfast.

THE INTELLECTUAL ON STAGE

Thomas Kilroy

The post-intellectual thing itself.

This is an attempt to say something about three Anglo-Irish playwrights whose work displays intellectuality, admittedly in very different ways — Beckett, Yeats and Shaw. I am going to work backwards, from Beckett to Yeats and Yeats to Shaw to try to illustrate what has been eliminated in Beckett: the social, the cultural, the representational, the reflection on stage of life outside the theatre. Shaw may be seen as the naturalist, the social realist, of the three but what is not often acknowledged is that, in this context, the attempt to escape from naturalistic theatre begins with Shaw in his later plays. The experiments there may not always work but the movement is towards fantasy and the surreal and the movement is intellectual.

In this discussion the quality of mind of the playwright is at least as important as the stage action, that which is being dramatized, upon the stage. In fact, the two are inextricable and what is being dramatized, permeating everything else, is the mind of the playwright in action.

This is a problematical area. Firstly, there is the problem of commerce and the fact that the intellectual playwright cannot be marketed. At the other end of the spectrum there is the conviction that the more visceral, the more spontaneous, the more unmediated the theatrical experience, the better. From this perspective intellectuality may appear to be a brake, or block, on creativity itself.

Theatre, too, is a collaborative art form in ways in which other art forms are not. Without the group there can be no theatre. Intellectual expression has to find its place in that group, if it is to survive. So, whatever else we are talking about here, we are not talking about the intellectual as theorist, the intellectual as essayist. In other words we are not talking about the common expression of the intellectual which is the imposition of a strong, single vision upon others, inviting response, yes, but with absolute conviction as to the validity of its own argument. I see intellectuality in the theatre as different, less dictatorial, something which takes its place, along with other kinds of expression, in a larger scheme of things.

There is one other feature of drama which may pose a conflict between intellectuality and staging. Drama is most often best served by direct simplicity, simplicity of form, simplicity of idea. Abstracted from even the most complex plays, this central idea may be expressed in a simple formula, what Yeats called "the single effect". Someone once said of Shaw that each of his plays could be reduced to a single epigram. There is an implied conflict here between simplicity of form and complexity of thought, which is one of the technical problems which faced each of these three playwrights.

The usual exploration of the intellect, on the other hand, doesn't always work in this way, through simplicity. The pull is in a different direction — not towards limiting the idea but towards its exhaustion in a growing density of meaning and an accumulating assembly of references. There are commentators, for instance, who would say that the expression of ideas in drama is necessarily superficial, that the intellectual burden of a play cannot be anything more than what an audience can absorb quickly and in a brief time span.

If all of this sounds problematical, what of the intellectual writer's reponse to it? Certainly there is a defensiveness on the part of some playwrights who feel the need to provide elaborate exegesis of their work in the form of explanatory essays. Shaw's vast body of prefaces is one example of this and it is clear from the importance which he attached to these prefaces that he considered them to be an intrinsic part of the plays themselves. Yeats, on the other hand, displays an admirable loftiness on the subject of the intellectual content of his plays. Intelligence, for Yeats, never needed a defence. But the most graphic example of an intellectual reaction of a playwright towards critical debate on his work is to be found in Beckett.

Beckett had a kind of wild comic method of dealing with questions of an intellectual nature in relation to his work. In the early 1950s he wrote two letters which illustrate this — one written just before, and one just after, the initial appearance on stage in Paris of *Waiting for Godot*.

The first letter was to Michel Polac, who was planning a broadcast of extracts from the play to try to promote a full-scale stage production. This was the great age of radio drama, when a writer like Ionescu could make his first appearance in English not on stage but over the airwaves. The radio production of *Waiting for Godot*, it was hoped, might expedite a stage production, which is, in fact, what happened.

The second letter was to the director of the first German production of the play, Carlheinz Caspari, when Beckett had already had the experience of seeing the play in performance in Paris. Both letters are typical of the exchanges which take place between a playwright and director of new work with this difference: Beckett is wholly anarchic on the subject of theatre. In answer to a query about his idea of theatre, he says that he is completely ignorant about theatre because he never goes to it. He goes on to say that he knows nothing about *Waiting for Godot* itself, that he is deeply suspicious of anyone who tries to find meaning in it and that he resists, strongly, any efforts at analysis of what is going on up on that stage.

There is, of course, a reason for such a strategy. Beckett was determined that his play reach its audience without interpretation, that the experience in the theatre be a frontal one of engagement with the thing itself, no more, no less. Something begins, something proceeds, something ends. Above all he resists the notion of theatre as representation. This does not represent something else, it is, to paraphrase Beckett himself on the subject of *Finnegans Wake*, it is the thing itself.

Here is the spare account of this from the first letter, the one to Polac:

I know no more about this play than anyone who manages to read it attentively.

I do not know in what spirit I wrote it.

I know no more of the characters than what they say, what they do and what happens to them. Of their appearance I must have indicated the little I have been able to make out. The bowler hats for example.

I do not know who Godot is. I do not even know if he exists. And I do not know if they believe he does, these two who are waiting for him.

By disowning knowledge, Beckett would appear to have divested himself of all intellectual intention in his play. But then, towards the end of the letter, he reveals his choice of positioning, which is at the centre of much intellectuality in theatre – that is, distancing, the cool removal of the author from the subject matter, the rising above the actual, the particular, to a position of supremely distanced perspective, in other words to a position of intellectual possession, intellectual shaping of the material. The position which Beckett achieves is an intellectual one, which gives him apparent freedom from thought itself. But if he arrives at this post-intellectual status, beyond the process of thought, he can only have arrived there by a profound process of thinking.

This distancing in Beckett is close to Yeats's discovery of Asiatic simplicity of staging and its distancing from the need to represent something outside the theatre.

> I hope [Yeats wrote in "Certain Noble Plays of Japan"] to have attained the distance from life which can make credible strange events, elaborate words. I have written a little play that can be played in a room … There will be no scenery.

This is also the stance which draws much of the hostility to ideas in the theatre, the unwarranted claim that the intellectual is too remote and lacking in feeling. This is simply a failure to recognize the depth of passion which can be conveyed through thinking. Here is Beckett again from that perch above the created play:

> I am no longer part of it, and never will be again. Estragon, Vladimir, Pozzo and Lucky, their time and space, I have been able to know a little about them by staying very far away from the need to understand.

In his second letter, the one to to the German director, on the identity of Godot, he offers one of those dizzy, comic turns of his: "If his name [Godot] suggests the heavens, it is only to the extent that a product to promote hair growth can seem heavenly."

One of the hazards facing the intellectual in writing a play is the temptation to intervene, to interpolate ideas into the script, to editorialize or otherwise express ideas that haven't earned their places in the action of the play. There are a couple of such moments in *Waiting for Godot* which raise this issue and it is worth reflecting on how Beckett triumphs over the problem.

One is Lucky's monologue in Act One, a savage, ironical display of the futility of all reasoning. Another is Vladimir's beautiful threnody with its dying fall towards the end of the play.

> Was I sleeping while the others suffered? Am I sleeping now? Tomorrow, when I wake, or think I do, what shall I say of today? That with Estragon my friend, at this place, until the fall of night, I waited for Godot? That Pozzo passed, with his carrier, and that he spoke to us? Probably. But in all that what truth will there be?

In addition to these two interventions, a possible third is Pozzo's distraught outburst on "accursed time", but that particular moment is more integrated into the preceding dialogue. The other two are different; they are surprising eruptions on the surface of banality and routine, moments of intense focus or anchorage in a flow of disconnectedness and absurdity, moments, in other words, where the mind of the author is fully on display.

By freeing the stage of representation Beckett gave himself immense freedom to surprise his audience. Surprise and the unexpected are ancient ingredients of theatre. In Beckett the surprises are intellectual, freed of the tyranny of knowledge and of the obligations of narrative.

There is a difficulty here for the actor. Actors like to find what they call "lines" in a play's development, for instance lines in character development, which allow them to build towards particular moments of intensity. They are uncomfortable with moments of intensity which appear to come out of nowhere. But Beckett's creatures are not characters in the conventional sense. They are usable figures in a setting which retains its staginess throughout. The stage remains a stage even after the first line is spoken, after the first steps have been taken from point A to point B.

In his letter to Caspari, Beckett himself was perfectly aware of this difficulty for the actor and director but he was also intellectually secure in his own ambitions. He is adamant that this is not a symbolist play, nor is it a play of forms and ideas. "First and foremost it is a question of something that happens, almost a routine, and it is this dayliness [sic] and this materiality, in my view, that needs to be brought out." On characterization he provides a breathtaking, intellectual lucidity that in one move undermines the whole, traditional idea of human identitiy on the stage.

> The characters are living creatures, only just living perhaps, they are not emblems. I can readily understand your unease at their lack of characterisation. But I would urge you to see in them less the result of an attempt at abstraction, something I am almost incapable of, than a refusal to tone down all that is at one and the same time complex and amorphous in them.

Then, like an afterthought, he offers the fortunate German director a consolation, derived from his own experience of seeing the first production in Paris, and in doing so he restores the creatures of his imagination to the human family. "If I may judge from our experience here in Paris, you will see identities shaping up as your work proceeds."

To move back from Beckett to Yeats and Shaw is to observe something of what Beckett has eliminated, including the conventional idea of characterization. He had his own opinions of Yeats and Shaw, a huge respect for the poet and a less than positive view of GBS. In yet another letter, on 1 June 1956, he responded to a request from the Irish actor Cyril Cusack to write a programme note, in French, no less, on Shaw, for a production at the Gaiety Theatre in Dublin. He puts Yeats, Synge and even O'Casey ahead of Mr Shaw. Here is his response to Cusack's request:

> This is too tall an order for me. I wouldn't write in French for King's Street. I wouldn't suggest that GBS is not a great play-wright, whatever that is when it's at home. What I would do is give the whole unupsettable apple-cart for a sup of the Hawk's Well, or the Saints', or a whiff of Juno, to go no further.

In truth all three of these playwrights are engaged in the elimination of naturalistic detail in order to clear space for the expression of intellect. Beckett is engaged in the elimination of received myth, which Yeats drew upon so heavily, replacing it with personal myth, a mythology of emptiness for the mid-twentieth century. Yeats, too, is engaged in the elimination of the naturalism which Shaw was so dependent on at the start of his career. "I have been thinking a good deal about plays lately", Yeats wrote in 1903, "and I have been wondering why I dislike the clear and logical construction which seems necessary if one is to succeed on the modern stage." You feel that he has to be thinking of the great success of Shaw: remember the nightmare which he had of Shaw appearing to him as a knitting machine in perpetual motion.

But Shaw, too, as he proceeded, tried to shift drama into a new dimension, as he does in Act Three of *Man and Superman* or in later plays like *Too True to Be Good*. The latter anticipated, and perhaps even influenced, later theatrical developments in the twentieth century.

In each of the three cases the aim is the same: to divest the stage of the furniture of the ordinary to create a free stage space to release the free play of intelligence. This free stage space is given meaning, not by reference to life offstage, but by the nature of events that happen onstage, as in the startling lines, setting the scene of Yeats's play *The Herne's Egg*:

This is Tara; in a moment
Men must come out of the gate

Like Beckett, Yeats considered conventional characterization an obstacle to this free expression. One can see why. The illusion of traditional characterization in the theatre is that we have before us a compex individuality, which includes the illusion of independence – independence, that is, of its author. Traditional characterization has the waywardness of real life, its unpredictability, with opinions that seem to arise out of the individuality of the character and not as a mouthpiece of the author.

In order to deal with this Yeats worked out a theory of stage characterization. It arises from his reflecting on the critical dogma "that if a play does not contain definite character, its constitution is not strong enough for the stage". He then, as always, goes back into the tradition of drama, where he suddenly finds illumination.

Suddenly it strikes us that character is continuously present in comedy alone, and there is much tragedy, that of Corneille, Racine, that of Greece and Rome, where its place is taken by passions and motives, one person being jealous, another full of love or remorse or pride or anger.

Passion, for Yeats, removes the tragic character from the attendant details of charcterization, to a place of stillness and silence, of what he calls "tragic reverie" where passion becomes wisdom – disembodied, beyond time. It is remarkable how often Yeats anticipates Beckett, as in his account of this tragic suspension portrayed in great painting "where we find there sadness and gravity, a certain emptiness even, as of a mind that waited the supreme crisis (and indeed it seems at times as if the graphic art, unlike poetry which sings the crisis itself, were the celebration of waiting)".

As we know, at a certain point Yeats withdrew altogether from public theatre, retreating to a form of private drama "distinguished, indirect, and symbolic, and having no need of mob or Press to pay its way – an aristocratic form". There are many possible responses to this, including outright rejection. But if we stay with Yeats on his own terms we see an achievement of bold intellectual ambition. One of the clearest descriptions of how this private drama might be presented is in the opening stage directions of the play *The Resurrection*.

Before I had finished this play I saw that its subject-matter might make it unsuited for the public stage in England or Ireland. I had begun it with an ordinary stage scene in the mind's eye, curtained walls, a window and door at back, a curtained door at left. I now changed the stage directions and wrote songs for the unfolding and folding of the curtain that it might be played in a studio or a drawing-room like my dance plays, or at the Peacock Theatre before a specially chosen audience.

In this short one-act play Yeats dramatizes nothing less than the collision of Christianity and Greco-Roman civilization. In the 1931 edition of the play his usable figures are labelled The Hebrew, The Syrian and The Greek, representing the the three main currents of early Western civililization. These are the carriers of the play's action, the voices who carry the interpreting intelligence behind the play.

If this were a play by Shaw we would have been offered a triangular debate between the three figures, on the nature of progress, perhaps, or on what constitutes the exceptional individual, the kind of person who makes a significant contribution to the evolution of the species. While Yeats's play is also highly verbal, it goes beyond language to ritual. The three figures enact a ritual of revelation, revelation of the violent, bloody moment which, in the Yeatsian vision, marks one cycle of history from another. This is the killing of a god and the consuming of his flesh and blood. Yeats was fascinated by such mystery-cults, seeing the Christian myth as part of the myths of death and resurrection of the cults of the dying god Attis, Adonis or Dionysus, devoured by his followers. His play ends with the apparition of the risen god with its beating heart. Belief in the supernatural is what, finally, distinguishes the Yeatsian theatre from that of Beckett and Shaw.

Even in the most Beckettian of these short plays of Yeats, *Purgatory*, the distinction from Beckett is pronounced. Many people have remarked upon how the play anticipates Beckett in the achieved simplicity of the figures in the scene: an old man, a boy, a ruined house, a bare tree. The profound difference, however, is that Yeats relies upon a complex, specific idea, that of cyclical repetition in life which imprisons the human as did the old device of Fate. Beckett freed himself from all such specifics.

The standard account of Shaw's development as a playwright would say that he begins as a nineteenth-century Ibsenite with the so-called problem or discussion plays like *Widowers' Houses* and *Mrs Warren's Profession*. Later he tried to move away from naturalism and sociology to a theatre of personal vision. Throughout, however, the essential Shavian stage device is the dramatic debate, a dialectic in which the process of thesis and anti-thesis is at least as important as synthesis, if there is one, "changing us", as Shaw put it, "from bewildered spectators of a monstrous confusion to men intelligently conscious of the world and its destinies". He believed that this intellectual conversion, as it were, of the audience, is the true business of the great playwrights and he lists them from Euripides to Ibsen. No doubt he would have included himself on the list.

One of the turning points in this development of Shaw is the Third Act of *Man and Superman*. The single, simple theatrical formula which Shaw returns to again and again is that of romantic comedy, the journey of a couple or couples towards marriage or the prospect of marriage, overcoming comic obstacles along the way, the most important one being inadequate self-knowledge. Jack Tanner and Ann Whitefield in *Man and Superman* fulfil this role with this crucial addition. Because they are creatures of what Shaw called the Life Force, they are swept by a power in nature that is greater than any human agency. The traditional, romantic-comic surrender of male to female or female to male at the end of this play becomes a powerful collapse which has some semblance to death. When Ann says to Tanner in that strange conclusion of their romance, "you very nearly killed me, Jack", she means it.

Shaw called the play, ominously, "a comedy and a philosophy". The philosophy comes mostly in Act Three of the play, where he transposes his finely detailed social drama into the hereafter, a benign hell of almost endless intellectual discussion complete with an easily offended Lucifer. All this is accomplished on stage with the aid of a new-fangled machine, the motor car. There are four characters. Tanner becomes Don Juan, Ann becomes Donna Ana and her father has been transmogrified into a talking statue. The fourth character, the Devil, is Tanner's antagonist in the debate but Ann and her father participate as well. The subjects covered in this most overt form of intellectual theatre include heaven and hell, obviously, the place of culture in English society, human evolution and the Life Force, militarism, the works of Dante and Milton, gender and civilization, together with several asides of a critical nature on the arts. It is a relentless assault on the patience of its audience. Far from Beckett and Yeats, the specific ideas rain down upon the stage and even the Devil complains about the length of the speeches.

It would be easy to conclude that this intellectuality of debating in Shaw is of a lesser order than the intellectuality of Yeats or Beckett, more mechanical, less subtle, more prosaic, less poetical. But it is also important to acknowledge that Shaw in his own way is also a visionary. This vision, too, is intellectual. *Too True to Be Good* opens with a patient in bed (and this is how she is referred to throughout – as the Patient). By the bedside sits a huge microbe of luminous jelly who looks like a monster from a science-fiction film. The microbe takes a lively part in the satirical, medical bedside scene that follows. The play itself is an angry, prophetic, apocalyptic, disillusioned drama masquerading as whimsical comedy. It reflects the deep disturbance in Europe between the wars. The comedy, like that of Beckett, is often close to despair. The problem with the play, like the late Shaw plays generally, is that, despite the surrealism, the science fiction, the fantasy, you feel Shaw never fully surrenders to the radical theatricality that he is toying with. His consuming interest in society is still here, the comic style is still that of the paradox and epigram of the early plays, and the relentless debates continue on and on like a tic out of control.

He was fully aware, however, of the difficulty of experiment in theatre. At the age of 79 he talked about the member of the audience in a programme note, as follows:

> He must be prepared to come across from time to time a sort of play which quite upsets his notions of what a play should be. He may not like it at first, but if it takes a grip of the stage, he must go on enduring it until he does like it.

He was defending his own late plays here but he might also have been addressing the troubled first audiences of *Waiting for Godot*, 20 years later, in Paris.

This was the Madden-Rooney Public Lecture at the University of Notre Dame, Dublin Seminar, 2012.

One of Ireland's leading playwrights, Thomas Kilroy was born in 1934 in Callan, Co Kilkenny and studied at University College, Dublin. He is the author of 16 plays for the stage, most recently Christ Deliver Us! *(2010), and one novel,* The Big Chapel *(Faber, 1971). He is Emeritus Professor of Modern English at NUI Galway, and a member of Aosdána. He lives in Kilmaine, Co Mayo.*

WAXING FROM NOTHING

—

Daniel Tobin

From nothing.

(Editor's Note: The following extract is from a book-length poem, From Nothing, *forthcoming in 2014.)*

Georges Lemaître (1894–1966), who fought in and survived many of the major battles of the First World War as well as the Nazi occupation of Europe during the Second, was a Belgian mathematician, theoretical physicist and Jesuit priest whose insights during the 1930s and 1940s provided solutions to physical problems stemming from Einstein's general theory of relativity and quantum mechanics that Einstein himself did not foresee. Though a lesser-known figure in cosmology, he was the first to develop a theory of an expanding universe through the explosion of a "primeval atom", what has become known as "the big bang". George Gamow (1904–1968) was a theoretical physicist and cosmologist, and early advocate of the Big Bang Theory.

Jubilant billowing from the choir loft, throngs in song,
the faithful processing through the chapel's threshold,
bearing with them the statue, image of the apparition –

the sun dancing in its window in the clouds, the sun
a burning halo raining petals, in the center of its seal
Joseph with infant Jesus, around them daylight stars.

"How can one avoid being skeptical, Coimbra seeing
nothing of the witness, of the events at Fatima?"
You, caught in the crosshairs of your paths to truth –

the piety of feasts, statistical notions, Masses and mass,
and energy immanent "in Galilean local coordinates"
while the universe speeds its breakneck transcendence,

the galaxies sanctuaries in recession without end.
So you saw lambda on the right hand not the left,
Einstein's crystalline sphere in pin-point balance

tipped from the equation – "The cosmological constant
may be compared to iron rods hidden inside a building,
indispensible to the structure of any synthesis more vast."

Saw photons decoupled into light in an instant's surge.
Saw horizons cooling and calibrated out of the fog.
Saw, before Oppenheimer, stars in radial collapse,

him leaving you un-cited. And the letter from Princeton
with the master's judgment: *I am unable to believe
that such an ugly thing should be realized in nature.*

———

To you nonetheless comes the invitation, to mingle
with Einstein, Gödel, Bohr, and so to enter life
inside the magic circle, its vivid talk, your star again

in ascent, though the good son sadly begs to decline –
that future eclipsed behind the orbit of your duty.
Turn, then, to Pascal's double infinity, infinite depth,

infinite immensity, and nature a Janus face of cold
extremes, vast extents, where mind drifts uncertainly,
and everything seen *an imperceptible dot* stretched

above *the greater nothingness beyond our reach* –
seeing in him your shadow double, mathematician,
priest, drawn by both to the *astonishing processes.*

Observe: to derive a solution to the problem of three
bodies, in space or scalar field, how the perturbation
of one in motion with the other is caused by the third.

Observe: geometry at the quantum level is nonlocal,
the Planck threshold a phase from which spacetime
emerges, before which no space no time, nowhere.

Observe: Contrary to Pascal, one cannot deduce God
from infinite nature. Better to prefer *deus absconditus,*
God supremely inaccessible, hidden, unknowable.

But from the unknowable, the known and its motion,
all in concert. *These extremes touch and join by going
in opposite directions, and meet in God, in God alone.*

———

All one, one would believe, and *Behind Every Door:
God* – the pope in his prayerful speech bearing witness
to the august instant of the primordial Fiat Lux,

*confirmation of the contingent universe from the hands
of the creator, well founded deduction, a bursting forth
from nothing into a sea of light, gesture of generous love.*

Never, it appears, will you live it down, Pius's piety
the confirming gaffe, your two paths confounded, confused, and you returned from Rome, bruising into class,

unlike (students noted) your irrepressibly cheerful self,
your primordial atom model still unproven by your lights,
curtailed, potentially, by an earlier stage of contraction

unaccounted for as yet in all the empirical data, in all
the exacting equations clarifying a lens on the known –
the phoenix universe you entertained, "very beautiful",

or the fact when wave functions collapse it's the eye
parsing the probable into the real, extemporizing all
possible outcomes, many worlds, the real it turns out

more prodigal than even Pascal's infinities, finitudes
roiling just beyond the glass edges of science and faith
in the bottoming abyss below before, now, and after

in which, in your time, you labor behind the scenes
to salvage the Truth, its necessity, its separateness —
the fraught message of telling your infallible pope no.

———

George Gamow

"Mary had a little lambda. His fleece was Jesus — Ha!
Of course, back in Odessa as a child, I had to discover
for myself, so I take communion in Orthodox Church,

run home with bread and wine secreted in my cheek,
place it under microscope — I see no transubstantiation.
That's experiment that made me, Gamow, a scientist.

Can you imagine, from hocus pocus to nucleosynthesis,
how in first five minutes light — dense particle soup —
recombines to form self, then bridges unbridgeable path

to make hydrogen, helium, all our heavier elements
without which no inflation, so no so called Big Bang,
since priest could not account for equal values — stretch

of cosmic rays across scope of universe from this mix
I call *ylem*, from Middle English word for substance.
When Pope says this or Pope says that I have great fun,

add chunks of speech to my own paper, watch eyebrows
rise, not God. But priest is excellent, better with math
than me, I admit, though he still believes in fairy tales.

It took an atheist to see what must remain at radio end
of spectrum, and how his swelling lambda came to be,
I who with my wife once braved Black Sea in a kayak

to escape Soviet Union — a failure. How I'll never forget
sight of this dolphin I glimpsed through a passing wave
illuminated, just then, by the sun sinking below horizon."

———

This process of coming to life, autocatalysis of wave
to particle, particle to wave, from indeterminacy,
such that the photons fuse, the sun shines, the clay,

crystalline in its shallow pool, flickers into motion
so that in time the observer might observe, so that
in mind's conjuring what had come to be must be

brought before the mind as though it had not been,
could not be, until fashioned from the probabilities,
and all that might have been, too, fanning out deeply.

*The theory says a lot, but does not really bring us any closer
to the secret of Der Alter*, "the Old One", so Einstein
confided to Born. And now the master's dead is he

gifted with the old one's secret, and your mother,
the windows of both their faces shaded and shut?
All goes onward and outward, nothing collapses — Whitman.

Except the wave function out of its eternal now
behind the proton's spin, before Planck's length waxes
from nothing, and nothing there until it's measured.

Who measures the dead? *For our perpetual vows
Canon Lemaître designed a brilliant course, how the life
of the mind carries the image of a nebula expanding,*

spirit formed in contact with matter, the world-lines
of our becoming a further transcendence promising
what follows. Pure miracle? No. A phase. A threshold.

Daniel Tobin was born in Brooklyn in 1958 and attended Iona College (BA), Harvard University (MA), the Program for Writers at Warren Wilson College (MFA), and The University of Virginia (PhD). He is the author of six books of poems, most recently Second Things, Belated Heavens *and* The Net, *forthcoming in 2014, all from Four Way Books. He has also authored two critical studies,* Passage to the Center: Imagination and the Sacred in the Poetry of Seamus Heaney *(University of Kentucky Press, 1999) and* Awake in America: On Irish-American Poetry *(University of Notre Dame Press, 2011), and has edited* The Book of Irish American Poetry from the Eighteenth Century to the Present *(University of Notre Dame Press, 2007),* Selected Early Poems of Lola Ridge *(Quale Press, 2007), and* Poet's Work, Poet's Play: Essays on the Practice and the Art *(University of Michigan Press, 2008). He is currently Interim Dean of the School of the Arts at Emerson College, Boston.*

REAGAN AND THE WALL OF SEPARATION: A VIEW FROM IRELAND (1985)

Hubert Butler

Constitutional memory.

The American elections are over. Have any before been watched so intently? Half the world has been sitting beside its television set and a new type of man has come into being to match the new technology. Reagan can project his complete personality, body, clothes, voice and appropriate gestures into a billion homes with his arguments, promises and rhetoric in the same package. Mondale claims he has been defeated largely by television, which in the hands of an expert reduces all politics into personalised snippets.

When, over two centuries ago, the thirteen American colonies were claiming their rights, Edmund Burke almost alone stood up for them. His two great speeches on American Taxation and on Conciliation must have taken a couple of hours each to deliver. He was a boring speaker with a bad manner and towards the end he was addressing almost empty benches. Yet in print these speeches have survived, many times reproduced, because on almost every page there is some penetrating observation about politics or human nature, whose relevance is not only for 1774–5 but for to-day.

Will posterity be able to rescue anything of the kind from the mountain of triviality that enveloped the Reagan victory? It was unique, because for the first time television had brought the fundamentalists out from their strongholds in the Bible Belt. They spread themselves over the network and all America was theirs. Even here in Ireland I have heard the principal Televangelist on a cassette. The Rev Jerry Falwell is the founder of "the Moral Majority" and he boasted that he could bring eight and a half million voters to the polls for Reagan and that he had "activated" millions more; "I think we will easily put 10–15 millions at the polls nation wide."

I keep in touch with the United States through my American son-in-law and before the election I received from Jerry Falwell, as did many thousands of Americans, a moving appeal to take part "with a million other Christians" in a Day of National Fasting and Prayer from sundown on Sunday, November 4 to sundown on November 5. We are to pray that on election day God will lead

Americans to vote for righteous men and women at all levels of government. He writes, "I am not talking about Democrats or Republicans." All the same it is fairly clear who the top-righteous man is. He has often been photographed with Jerry Falwell at prayer breakfasts and other religious occasions.

Counterattacking, Mondale's supporters circulated a Petition to President Reagan, which recipients were to sign. As it was concise I will quote it in full:

> The Founding Fathers of America made a wise choice about the Separation of Church and State and the prohibition against the establishment of Religion by the government. Hundreds of years of bloody religious warfare and persecution in Europe led them to write the Constitution as they did.
>
> For over two hundred years America's religious institutions and the religious liberty of its people have flourished without government endorsement or advocacy of their viewpoints. This, the American Way, has proved best for all of us.
>
> I am alarmed by your recent efforts to inject ultra-fundamentalist Christian doctrine into the laws and policies governing all of America's citizens. I urge you to reconsider your position on these complex issues. The Presidency is an office of all the people, not a forum for one particular dogma.

What in fact are Jerry Falwell's religious views? They are probably much like those of Ian Paisley, who is on the board of a large university at Greenville, South Carolina in the Bible Belt. Falwell, as Chancellor of a Baptist college at Lynchburg, Virginia, lately told an interviewer that all his faculty members have to sign a statement of faith in the inerrancy of the scriptures and the biblical account of the Creation. He believes he has a divine mission to christianise America and, with Reagan's support, he is heading an attack on the decisions of the Supreme Court during the sixties, when the Justices interpreted the Separation of Church and State with the utmost strictness. Falwell's main target is the 1962 decision banning religious devotions in public schools and the 1973 decision to legalise abortion. These are sensitive issues and the fundamentalists have not hesitated to call their opponents atheists and murderers.

Reagan's way of handling Jefferson's Wall of Separation is to ignore it:

> The truth is, politics and morality are inseparable and morality's foundation is religion; religion and politics are necessarily related.

We need religion as a guide.

To what religion is he referring? There are some 280 different sects in the USA, and at least seventy million who belong to no church at all. Reagan himself was raised as a Disciple of Christ but became a Presbyterian and we saw him attend a Catholic church in Ballyporeen. He does not go to church in the USA, because, say his aides, the necessary security precautions might disturb other worshippers. He has endeared himself to the fundamentalists by his belief that the biblical account of the Creation should have equal authority in the schools with the theory of Evolution and by his obsessions about the imminence of Armageddon, that great battle between Good and Evil, which will be fought before the Day of Judgement. He has no doubt where the Powers of Evil are to be found.

The anti-abortion campaign threatens to be bitterly divisive. To the anti-abortionists it is as crucial an issue to-day as slavery in the last century. Their opponents compare it to Prohibition, which became law in 1919 only to be repealed as unworkable fourteen years later.

The Justices of the Supreme Court hold their office for life, so that popular pressure cannot influence their decisions. Fortunately for Reagan, five of the nine are over seventy-five, so he may be able to replace one or two of them with men favorable to the mandatory school prayer and to the banning of abortion.

It is clear that in the USA, as in Ireland, the fundamentalists are more politically assertive than the mainstream Protestants, who mostly cherish the Separation of Church and State and, while condemning abortion, have no wish to make it illegal. A characteristic statement came from Bishop Paul Moore of the Episcopal Diocese of New York, who believes that "the soul of America has gone wrong." He said, "The nation was being conned into false judgement by the slick veneer of religious verbiage." Of school prayers, he said:

> If a school becomes a place where children are taught to pray, it is
> a short step to their thinking of the State as an instrument of God
> and that leads to the most demonic of all Church-State confusions,
> a tendency to mingle patriotic and religious fervour.

He saw a dearth of compassion and serious thought:

> Abortion is an issue not to be dictated by governments. If a woman

is considering one, her decision is one of the most agonising and painful she will ever address. She needs to have freedom to work through her decision.

There is an unspoken question here. Is Ronald Reagan one of the silliest and most dangerous of all American presidents? Or is he merely an astute politician, who has captured the South from the Democrats by his "slick veneer of religious verbiage"?

I was in America in 1962, when the Supreme Court made the decision, which Ronald Reagan and Jerry Falwell now wish to revoke. The Justices, voting eight to one, declared the recital of a state prayer in the public schools to be unconstitutional. It was a very short prayer and seemed innocuous and undenominational, but when four parents, Unitarian, Jewish, Agnostic and Ethical Culture objected, the Supreme Court upheld their objection. Justice Black, who delivered the opinion, quoted President Madison in justification:

> There are more instances of abridgment of the freedom of the people by gradual and silent encroachments of those in power than by violent and sudden usurpations. It is proper to take alarm at the first experiment on our liberties. Who does not see that the same authority which can establish Christianity in exclusion of all other religions may establish with the same ease any particular sect of Christianity in exclusion of all other sects.

He recalled the circumstances which had induced the Founding Fathers to erect their Wall of Separation. Though they were for the most part classically educated country gentlemen, they had been real revolutionaries. They upset many century-old traditions and overthrew at least eight established churches. The Church of England was established in New York, Virginia, Maryland, the two Carolinas and Georgia, Congregationalism in Massachusetts, New Hampshire and Connecticut. In some states there was discrimination against Catholics.

The men who drew up the Constitution and its amendments were aware that those, who have suffered religious persecution, often become the most experienced persecutors. Twenty years after the Pilgrim Fathers had fled from English bigotry to Massachusetts, they were themselves expelling Quakers, Catholics and others under pain of cruel punishment and even death. Nor can the Framers of the Constitution have been surprised by the fury they aroused in the churches they disestablished. Would Jefferson, an Anglican himself, have succeeded in disestablishing the tax-supported Anglican Church in Virginia if their clergy had not for the most part sided with Britain and left their parishes when war broke out?

Jefferson justified the intransigence of the Founding Fathers by a clause in the preamble to the Statute of Virginia for Religious Freedom. Abridged a little, it runs:

> Almighty God hath created the mind free ... (But) the impious presumption of legislators and rulers, civil as well as ecclesiastical, who being themselves but fallible and uninspired men have assumed dominion over the faith of others, setting up their own opinions and modes of thinking as the only true and infallible and as such endeavoring to impose them on others, hath established and maintained false religions over the greatest part of the world and through all time ... To compel a man to furnish contributions of money for the propagation of opinions which he disbelieves is sinful and tyrannical.

Jefferson himself, like Benjamin Franklin, was a Deist, but said he would been a Unitarian, had there been a Unitarian Church in Charlottesville. Of all the Founding Fathers, he was the one most concerned with religion and the freedom of religion. He wrote of Jesus that "he presented to us a system of morals the most perfect and sublime that has ever been taught to man ... To the corruption of Christianity I am indeed opposed but not to the genuine precepts of Jesus himself." He was part-author of the First Amendment, which runs: "Congress shall make no laws respecting the establishment of religion or prohibiting the free exercise thereof." The precise meaning of this has often been disputed. Jefferson himself interpreted it in the following way in his *Notes on Virginia*:

> The legitimate powers of government extend to such acts only as are injurious to others. But it does me no injury for my neighbor to say there are twenty gods or no god.

This is very far from Reagan's claim that "religion and politics are necessarily related".

Time has fully justified the Founding Fathers. No country in the world has been so free from religious conflict. Nowhere has religion been so freely practised. Yet Jefferson was as unpopular in his day as those who defend the Wall of Separation now. In 1962 Justice Black and his colleagues were told they were atheists in league with Moscow. Yet on the whole the churches and the leading newspapers approved. Cardinal Spellman protested but President Kennedy said the children will just have to pray that much more at home. The Catholic Church has often had some difficulty in meeting the Wall. There was a famous occasion in 1949, when Cardinal Spellman told Mrs Roosevelt she was unworthy to be an American mother, because she had approved of the Barden Bill by which federal money was to be devoted to public schools and secular schools only. The bill, he said, represented "a craven crusade of religious prejudice against the Catholic child and his inalienable rights".

The most telling criticism of the 1962 decision concerned expediency. Could the Supreme Court afford to take so many unpopular measures? The survival of the Court is more important than any single one of its measures. The Wall of Separation has often been breached. Does not the state provide chaplains for the army and compulsory chapel for West Point cadets? Would it not have been prudent to fob off the four parents somehow?

The answer is that the United States was founded on non-conformity and its leaders are pledged to protect the rights of the individual who will not conform. Time and again the One has overturned the smooth and settled orthodoxies of the Many. Sometimes he is a believer, as when some Jehovah's Witnesses refused to salute the American flag because it was "a graven image". Sometimes he is an unbeliever, as when Mrs Vashti McCollum successfully challenged the "released time" system of Bible classes in Illinois public schools, on behalf of her son, Jim, who had been brought up an agnostic. If the most insignificant of West Point cadets were to claim that compulsory chapel was unconstitutional, the Supreme Court might feel obligated to support him. It would no doubt be the end of his military career but it would also be the end of compulsory chapel.

In no country in the world are there so many religious organisations, all of them voluntary and functioning without interferences from the state. But the Wall of Separation, which protects their liberty, also defines its extent. All America is theirs to evangelise, but the law, as interpreted by the Supreme Court, enjoins that they must not ask a single cent from public funds or a single minute from a public servant's time for the diffusion or the defence of a private belief.

Hubert Butler (1900–1991) was twentieth-century Ireland's most distinguished essayist. He was the author of four collections of essays assembled in the last decade of his life and published by The Lilliput Press in Dublin: Escape from the Anthill *(1986),* The Children of Drancy *(1988),* Grandmother and Wolfe Tone *(1990) and* In the Land of Nod *(1996). Two new editions of his work,* The Eggman and the Fairies: Irish Essays *and* The Invader Wore Slippers: European Essays*, both edited by John Banville, were published by Notting Hill Editions in 2012. A fifth volume of unpublished essays,* The Appleman and the Poet, *including the one above, will appear in late 2013, again from The Lilliput Press.*

———

BUTLER ON THE WALL OF SEPARATION: RELEVANCE AND PROVENANCE

———

Richard Crampton

A continuing threat.

Butler wrote the above essay in 1985 after Reagan's election to a second term as President. It expands his earlier observations in "American Impressions: In Salt Lake City" (1962) and "The Bob Jones University" (1977), both included in his third collection of essays, *Grandmother and Wolfe Tone* (1990). The essay has previously appeared in *The Journal of the Butler Society 2010* (Vol 5, No 1, 2010) and in the *Princeton University Library Chronicle* (Vol 71, No 1, 2010). Butler and I edited it in 1985.

Butler hung a copy of *The Declaration of Independence* in his house, Maidenhall, in 1963. When he visited his daughter's family in Charlottesville, Virginia in 1972 and 1974, he read *The Federalist Papers* of Madison, Hamilton and Jay. He perused *The Constitution of the United States*, *The Bill of Rights* and Jefferson's *Notes on Virginia*. He visited Monticello, Jefferson's estate, and worked at the library of the University of Virginia founded by Jefferson.

For the classicist Butler, The Commonwealth of Virginia's motto *Sic Semper Tyrannis* fits the spirit of his essay. As Maurice Craig succinctly put it: "For all his elegance, Hubert Butler is no belle lettrist. For him an essay is a projectile, aimed at a particular target and freighted with what it needs to do its work: no more and no less. All his projectiles tend to converge on the same area of moral choice: the responsibilities of the individual to his community, and, by implication, those of the community towards him, in the special sphere where belief and conduct, dogma and decency, are so often in conflict" (Foreword, *Escape From The Anthill*, 1986).

———

Butler's theses reverberate today. He judiciously dissects the dangers of mixing religion, politics and government. Not only does this essay illuminate worldwide perturbations and atrocities in the twentieth and twenty-first centuries, both before and after his death – but it also anticipates those continuing threats to the American Wall of Separation he so carefully examined a generation ago, and which now flourish, much magnified by the social media.

The late journalist Joe Bageant (author of *Deer Hunting with Jesus: Dispatches from America's Class War*, Portobello Books, 2008) pointed out that Christian fundamentalists, including students, constitute 25 per cent of those entitled to vote in American state and national elections. Roughly twenty of the fifty million of these American fundamentalists voted in the 2000 and 2004 elections. A Gallup poll disclosed that a quarter to a third of the American population identifies itself as "born-again" evangelical. Most stand apart from mainstream America in their aspiration to scrap the Constitution and institute a "Biblical Law", such as the rules of the Old Testament. Like many of their Scots-Irish ancestors, they wish to create a theocratic state. The Religious Right always claim America was founded as a Christian nation. In his book, Bageant cites Frederick Clarkson, who agrees with Butler's perceptions, and (in his own classic *Eternal Hostility: The Struggle Between Theocracy and Democracy*, Common Courage Press, 1997) observes that the Religious Right "seek to restore a theocratic order that never was, not since the ratification of The Constitution. The Framers of The Constitution overthrew 150 years of colonial theocracies and theocratic wannabes. And when it was accomplished, Benjamin Franklin said, 'You have a republic if you can keep it'. So let's keep it."

Butler's concerns about theocrats eroding the Wall of Separation continue to be amply justified. Christian fundamentalists participate vigorously in contemporary social media. Dr Aaron Tabor's *Facebook Page for Jesus, With Highly Active Fans* posts the words of Jesus four or five times daily; *The Jesus Daily* has 8.2 million fans with several million interactions per week; *The Bible Presented by the United Bible Societies*, out of Reading, England, has eight million users. Will Facebook and other social media change how people worship? Thirty-one per cent of American Facebook users and twenty-four per cent of users outside the United States list religion in their profiles. Over 43 million Facebook users have at least one page categorized as religious. Will worship via social media so popularize and politicize religion that we can anticipate new threats to the Wall of Separation, as perceived by Butler in Reagan's 1984 campaign rhetoric? Indeed we can. These threats are precisely those identified by Butler nearly 30 years ago.

For example, Butler anticipates the case of Blake Page, an atheist cadet, who resigned six months before graduation from the publicly funded United States Military Academy at West Point. He could no longer bear widespread discriminatory bullying by faculty officers and fellow cadets. He identified the problem as the "unconstitutional proselytism" of evangelical Christianity. Yet Page did not contest his resignation legally, so it was never examined by the United States Supreme Court.

As of 2013, Butler's prescient disquiet about threats to the Wall of Separation rests no less on solid bedrock. The biased rhetoric and theocratic agendas of the six Republican presidential contenders in 2012 (Bachmann, Gingrich, Paul, Perry, Romney and Santorum) were imbued with fundamentalist, Catholic and Mormon beliefs. Despite Romney's ultimate defeat, very wealthy threats to The Wall of Separation abound. The fundamentalist Jerry Falwell, Jr Ministries, along with his Liberty University and the related Liberty Counsel, and Pat Robertson's Christian Broadcasting Network and Regent University, yearly take in nearly a billion dollars. Eight like-minded organizations of the Religious Right add over $200 million. This massive billion-plus dollar war-chest pours into the evangelical Christian crusade to insert creationism into public schools, to deny raped women abortions, and to block civil marriages for same-sex partners, all in the name of God's will. As Butler so elegantly discerned, such religious and gender-based threats constitute a real menace to the rights embodied in the First Amendment of the Constitution.

Richard Crampton, Hubert Butler's son-in-law, is Distinguished Professor of Medicine at the University of Virginia. With Antony Farrell of The Lilliput Press, he edited the second edition of Butler's Ten Thousand Saints: A Study of Irish and European Origins *(1974, 2011), reinforcing that book's hypotheses and conclusions about Irish oral prehistory with new scientific developments in genome-mapping and DNA-sampling.*

IT ALL TURNS ON AFFECTION

Wendell Berry

Boomers and stickers.

*"Because a thing is going strong now, it need not go strong for ever",
[Margaret] said. "This craze for motion has only set in during the last
hundred years. It may be followed by a civilization that won't be a
movement, because it will rest upon the earth."*
(E.M. Forster, *Howards End,* 1910)

One night in the winter of 1907, at what we have always called "the home
place" in Henry County, Kentucky, my father, then six years old, sat with his
older brother and listened as their parents spoke of the uses they would have
for the money from their 1906 tobacco crop. The crop was to be sold at
auction in Louisville on the next day. They would have been sitting in the
light of a kerosene lamp, close to the stove, warming themselves before
bedtime. They were not wealthy people. I believe that the debt on their
farm was not fully paid, there would have been interest to pay, there would
have been other debts. The depression of the 1890s would have left them
burdened. Perhaps, after the income from the crop had paid their
obligations, there would be some money that they could spend as they
chose. At around two o'clock the next morning, my father was wakened by
a horse's shod hooves on the stones of the driveway. His father was leaving
to catch the train to see the crop sold.

He came home that evening, as my father later would put it, "without
a dime". After the crop had paid its transportation to market and the
commission on its sale, there was nothing left. Thus began my father's
lifelong advocacy, later my brother's and my own, and now my daughter's
and my son's, for small farmers and for land-conserving economies.

———

The economic hardship of my family and of many others, a century ago, was
caused by a monopoly, the American Tobacco Company, which had
eliminated all competitors and thus was able to reduce as it pleased the

prices it paid to farmers. The American Tobacco Company was the work of James B. Duke of Durham, North Carolina, and New York City, who, disregarding any other consideration, followed a capitalist logic to absolute control of his industry and, incidentally, of the economic fate of thousands of families such as my own.

My effort to make sense of this memory and its encompassing history has depended on a pair of terms used by my teacher, Wallace Stegner. He thought rightly that we Americans, by inclination at least, have been divided into two kinds: "boomers" and "stickers". Boomers, he said, are "those who pillage and run", who want "to make a killing and end up on Easy Street", whereas stickers are "those who settle, and love the life they have made and the place they have made it in" (*Where the Bluebird Sings to the Lemonade Springs*, 1992). "Boomer" names a kind of person and a kind of ambition that is the major theme, so far, of the history of the European races in our country. "Sticker" names a kind of person and also a desire that is, so far, a minor theme of that history, but a theme persistent enough to remain significant and to offer, still, a significant hope.

The boomer is motivated by greed, the desire for money, property, and therefore power. James B. Duke was a boomer, if we can extend the definition to include pillage *in absentia*. He went, or sent, wherever the getting was good, and he got as much as he could take.

Stickers on the contrary are motivated by affection, by such love for a place and its life that they want to preserve it and remain in it. Of my grandfather I need to say only that he shared in the virtues and the faults of his kind and time, one of his virtues being that he was a sticker. He belonged to a family who had come to Kentucky from Virginia, and who intended to go no farther. He was the third in his paternal line to live in the neighborhood of our little town of Port Royal, and he was the second to own the farm where he was born in 1864 and where he died in 1946.

We have one memory of him that seems, more than any other, to identify him as a sticker. He owned his farm, having bought out the other heirs, for more than fifty years. About forty of those years were in hard times, and he lived almost continuously in the distress of debt. Whatever has happened in what economists call "the economy", it is generally true that the land economy has been discounted or ignored. My grandfather lived his life in an economic shadow. In an urbanizing and industrializing age, he was the wrong kind of man. In one of his difficult years he plowed a field on the lower part of a long slope and planted it in corn. While the soil was exposed, a heavy rain fell and the field was seriously eroded. This was heartbreak for my grandfather, and he devoted the rest of his life first to healing the scars and then to his obligation of care. In keeping with the sticker's commitment, he neither left behind the damage he had done nor forgot about it, but stayed to repair it, insofar as soil loss can be repaired. My father, I think, had his father's error in mind when he would speak of farmers attempting, always uselessly if not tragically, "to plow their way out of debt". From that time, my grandfather and my father were soil conservationists, a commitment that they handed on to my brother and to me.

———

It is not beside the point, or off my subject, to notice that these stories and their meanings have survived because of my family's continuing connection to its home place. Like my grandfather, my father grew up on that place and served as its caretaker. It has now belonged to my brother for many years, and he in turn has been its caretaker. He and I have lived as neighbors, allies, and friends. Our long conversation has often taken its themes from the two stories I have told, because we have been continually reminded of them by our home neighborhood and topography. If we had not lived there to be reminded and to remember, nobody would have remembered. If either of us had lived elsewhere, both of us would have known less. If both of us, like most of our generation, had moved away, the place with its memories would have been lost to us and we to it – and certainly my thoughts about agriculture, if I had thought of it at all, would have been much more approximate than they have been.

Because I have never separated myself from my home neighborhood, I cannot identify myself to myself apart from it. I am fairly literally flesh of its flesh. It is present in me, and to me, wherever I go. This undoubtedly accounts for my sense of shock when, on my first visit to Duke University, and by surprise, I came face to face with James B. Duke in his dignity, his glory perhaps, as the founder of that university. He stands imperially in bronze in front of a Methodist chapel aspiring to be a cathedral. He holds between two fingers of his left hand a bronze cigar. On one side of his pedestal is the legend: INDUSTRIALIST. On the other side is another single word: PHILANTHROPIST. The man thus commemorated seemed to me terrifyingly ignorant, even terrifyingly innocent, of the connection between his industry and his philanthropy. But I did know the connection. I felt it instantly and physically. The connection was my grandparents and thousands of others more or less like them. If you can appropriate for little or nothing the work and hope of enough such farmers, then you may dispense the grand charity of "philanthropy".

After my encounter with the statue, the story of my grandfather's 1906 tobacco crop slowly took on a new dimension and clarity in my mind. I still remembered my grandfather as himself, of course, but I began to think of him also as a kind of man standing in thematic opposition to a man of an entirely different kind. And I could see finally that between these two kinds there was a failure of imagination that was ruinous, that belongs indelibly to our history, and that has continued, growing worse, into our own time.

———

The term "imagination" in what I take to be its truest sense refers to a mental faculty that some people have used and thought about with the utmost seriousness. The sense of the verb "to imagine" contains the full richness of the verb "to see". To imagine is to see most clearly, familiarly, and understandingly with the eyes, but also to see inwardly, with "the mind's eye". It is to see, not passively, but with a force of vision and even with visionary force. To take it seriously we must give up at once any notion that imagination is disconnected from reality or truth or knowledge. It has nothing to do either with clever imitation of appearances or with "dreaming up". It does not depend upon one's attitude or point of view, but grasps securely the qualities of things seen or envisioned.

I will say, from my own belief and experience, that imagination thrives on contact, on tangible connection. For humans to have a responsible relationship to the world, they must imagine their places in it. To have a place, to live and belong in a place, to live from a place without destroying it, we must imagine it. By imagination we see it illuminated by its own unique character and by our love for it. By imagination we recognize with sympathy the fellow members, human and nonhuman, with whom we share our place. By that local experience we see the need to grant a sort of preemptive sympathy to all the fellow members, the neighbors, with whom we share the world. As imagination enables sympathy, sympathy enables affection. And it is in affection that we find the possibility of a neighborly, kind, and conserving economy.

Obviously there is some risk in making affection the pivot of an argument about economy. The charge will be made that affection is an emotion, merely "subjective", and therefore that all affections are more or less equal: people may have affection for their children and their automobiles, their neighbors and their weapons. But the risk, I think, is only that affection is personal. If it is not personal, it is nothing; we don't, at least, have to worry about governmental or corporate affection. And one of the endeavors of human cultures, from the beginning, has been to qualify and direct the influence of emotion. The word "affection" and the terms of value that cluster around it – love, care, sympathy, mercy, forbearance, respect, reverence – have histories and meanings that raise the issue of worth. We should, as our culture has warned us over and over again, give our affection to things that are true, just, and beautiful. When we give affection to things that are destructive, we are wrong. A large machine in a large, toxic, eroded cornfield is not, properly speaking, an object or a sign of affection.

———

My grandfather knew, urgently, the value of money, but only of such comparatively small sums as would have paid his debts and allowed to his farm and his family a decent prosperity. He certainly knew of the American Tobacco Company. He no doubt had read and heard of James B. Duke, and could identify him as the cause of a hard time, but nothing in his experience could have enabled him to imagine the life of the man himself.

James B. Duke came from a rural family in the tobacco country of North Carolina. In his early life he would have known men such as my grandfather. But after he began his rise as an industrialist, the life of a small tobacco grower would have been to him a negligible detail incidental to an opportunity for large profits. In the minds of the "captains of industry", then and now, the people of the land economies have been reduced to statistical numerals. Power deals "efficiently" with quantities that affection cannot recognize.

It may seem plausible to suppose that the head of the American Tobacco Company would have imagined at least that a dependable supply of raw material to his industry would depend upon a stable, reasonably thriving population of farmers and upon the continuing fertility of their farms. But he imagined no such thing. In this he was like apparently all agribusiness executives. They don't imagine farms or farmers. They imagine perhaps nothing at all, their minds being filled to capacity by numbers leading to the bottom line. Though the corporations, by law, are counted as persons, they do not have personal minds, if they can be said to have minds. It is a great oddity that a corporation, which properly speaking has no self, is by definition selfish, responsible only to itself. This is an impersonal, abstract selfishness, limitlessly acquisitive, but unable to look so far ahead as to preserve its own sources and supplies. The selfishness of the fossil-fuel industries by nature is self-annihilating; but so, always, has been the selfishness of the agribusiness corporations. Land, as Wes Jackson has said, has thus been made as exhaustible as oil or coal.

———

There is another difference between my grandfather and James B. Duke that may finally be more important than any other, and this was a difference of kinds of pleasure. We may assume that, as a boomer, moving from one chance of wealth to another, James B. Duke wanted only what he did not yet have. If it is true that he was in this way typical of his kind, then his great pleasure was only in prospect, which excludes affection as a motive.

My grandfather, on the contrary, and despite his life's persistent theme of hardship, took a great and present delight in the modest good that was at hand: in his place and his affection for it, in its pastures, animals, and crops, in favorable weather.

He did not participate in the least in what we call "mobility". He died, after 82 years, in the same spot he was born in. He was probably in his sixties when he made the one longish trip of his life. He went with my father southward across Kentucky and into Tennessee. On their return, my father asked him what he thought of their journey. He replied: "Well, sir, I've looked with all the eyes I've got, and I wouldn't trade the field behind my barn for every inch I've seen."

In such modest joy in a modest holding is the promise of a stable, democratic society, a promise not to be found in "mobility": our forlorn modern progress toward something indefinitely, and often unrealizably, better. A principled dissatisfaction with whatever one has promises nothing or worse.

James B. Duke would not necessarily have thought so far of the small growers as even to hold them in contempt. The Duke trust exerted an oppression that was purely economic, involving a mechanical indifference, the indifference of a grinder to what it grinds. It was not, that is to say, a political oppression. It did not *intend* to victimize its victims. It simply followed its single purpose of the highest possible profit, and ignored the "side effects". Confronting that purpose, any small farmer is only one, and one lost, among a great multitude of others, whose work can be quickly transformed into a great multitude of dollars.

Corporate industrialism has tended to be, and as its technological and financial power has grown it has tended increasingly to be, indifferent to its sources in what Aldo Leopold called "the land-community": the land, all its features and "resources", and all its members, human and nonhuman, including of course the humans who do, for better or worse, the work of land use (*A Sand County Almanac*, 1966). Industrialists and industrial economists have assumed, with permission from the rest of us, that land and people can be divorced without harm. If farmers come under adversity from high costs and low prices, then they must either increase their demands upon the land and decrease their care for it, or they must sell out and move to town, and this is supposed to involve no ecological or economic or social cost. Or if there are such costs, then they are rated as "the price of progress" or "creative destruction".

But land abuse *cannot* brighten the human prospect. There is in fact no distinction between the fate of the land and the fate of the people. When one is abused, the other suffers. The penalties may come quickly to a farmer who destroys perennial cover on a sloping field. They *will* come sooner or later to a land-destroying civilization such as ours.

And so it has seemed to me less a choice than a necessity to oppose the boomer enterprise with its false standards and its incomplete accounting, and to espouse the cause of stable, restorative, locally adapted economies of mostly family-sized farms, ranches, shops, and trades. Naïve as it may sound now, within the context of our present faith in science, finance, and technology – the faith equally of "conservatives" and "liberals" – this cause nevertheless has an authentic source in the sticker's hope to abide in and to live from some chosen and cherished small place – which, of course, is the agrarian vision that Thomas Jefferson spoke for, a sometimes-honored human theme, minor and even fugitive, but continuous from ancient times until now. Allegiance to it, however, is not a conclusion but the beginning of thought.

———

The problem that ought to concern us first is the fairly recent dismantling of our old understanding and acceptance of human limits. For a long time we knew that we were not, and could never be, "as gods". We knew, or retained the capacity to learn, that our intelligence could get us into trouble that it could not get us out of. We were intelligent enough to know that our intelligence, like our world, is limited. We seem to have known and feared the possibility of irreparable damage. But beginning in science and engineering, and continuing, by imitation, into other disciplines, we have progressed to the belief that humans are intelligent enough, or soon will be, to transcend all limits and to forestall or correct all bad results of the misuse of intelligence. Upon this belief rests the further belief that we can have "economic growth" without limit.

Economy in its original – and, I think, its proper – sense refers to household management. By extension, it refers to the husbanding of all the goods by which we live. An authentic economy, if we had one, would define and make, on the terms of thrift and affection, our connections to nature and to one another. Our present industrial system also makes those connections, but by pillage and indifference. Most economists think of this arrangement as "the economy". Their columns and articles rarely if ever mention the land-communities and land-use economies. They never ask, in their professional oblivion, why we are willing to do permanent ecological and cultural damage "to strengthen the economy?"

In his essay "Notes on Liberty and Property", Allen Tate gave us an indispensable anatomy of our problem. His essay begins by equating not liberty and property, but liberty and *control* of one's property. He then makes the crucial distinction between ownership that is merely legal and what he calls "effective ownership". If a property, say a small farm, has one owner, then the one owner has an effective and assured, if limited, control over it as long as he or she can afford to own it, and is free to sell it or use it, and (I will add) free to use it poorly or well. It is clear also that effective ownership of a small property is personal and therefore can, at least possibly, be intimate, familial, and affectionate. If, on the contrary, a person owns a small property of stock in a large corporation, then that person has surrendered control of the property to larger shareholders. The drastic mistake our people made, as Tate believed and I agree, was to be convinced "that there is *one* kind of property – just *property*, whether it be a thirty-acre farm in Kentucky or a stock certificate in the United States Steel Corporation". By means of this confusion, Tate said, "Small ownership … has been worsted by big, dispersed ownership – the giant corporation" (*Who Owns America?*, 1936). (It is necessary to append to this argument the further fact that by now, owing largely to corporate influence, land ownership implies the right to destroy the land-community entirely, as in surface mining, and to impose, as a consequence, the dangers of flooding, water pollution, and disease upon communities downstream.)

Tate's essay was written for the anthology *Who Owns America?*, the publication of which was utterly without effect. With other agrarian writings before and since, it took its place on the far margin of the national dialogue, dismissed as anachronistic, retrogressive, nostalgic, or (to use Tate's own term of defiance) reactionary in the face of the supposedly "inevitable" dominance of corporate industrialism. *Who Owns America?* was published in the Depression year of 1936. It is at least ironic that talk of "effective property" could have been lightly dismissed at a time when many rural people who had migrated to industrial cities were returning to their home farms to survive.

In 1936, when to the dominant minds a 30-acre farm in Kentucky was becoming laughable, Tate's essay would have seemed irrelevant as a matter of course. At that time, despite the Depression, faith in the standards and devices of industrial progress was nearly universal and could not be shaken.

———

But now, three-quarters of a century later, we are no longer talking about theoretical alternatives to corporate rule. We are talking with practical urgency about an obvious need. Now the two great aims of industrialism – replacement of people by technology and concentration of wealth into the hands of a small plutocracy – seem close to fulfillment. At the same time the *failures* of industrialism have become too great and too dangerous to deny. Corporate industrialism itself has exposed the falsehood that it ever was inevitable or that it ever has given precedence to the common good. It has failed to sustain the health and stability of human society. Among its characteristic signs are destroyed communities, neighborhoods, families, small businesses, and small farms. It has failed just as conspicuously and more dangerously to conserve the wealth and health of nature. No amount of fiddling with capitalism to regulate and humanize it, no pointless rhetoric on the virtues of capitalism or socialism, no billions or trillions spent on "defense" of the "American dream" can for long disguise this failure. The evidences of it are everywhere: eroded, wasted, or degraded soils; damaged or destroyed ecosystems; extinction of species; whole landscapes defaced, gouged, flooded, or blown up; pollution of the whole atmosphere and of the water cycle; "dead zones" in the coastal waters; thoughtless squandering of fossil fuels and fossil waters, of mineable minerals and ores; natural health and beauty replaced by a heartless and sickening ugliness. Perhaps its greatest success is an astounding increase in the destructiveness, and therefore the profitability, of war.

In 1936, moreover, only a handful of people were thinking about sustainability. Now, reasonably, many of us are thinking about it. The problem of sustainability is simple enough to state. It requires that the fertility cycle of birth, growth, maturity, death, and decay — what Albert Howard called "the Wheel of Life" — should turn continuously in place, so that the law of return is kept and nothing is wasted. For this to happen in the stewardship of humans, there must be a cultural cycle, in harmony with the fertility cycle, also continuously turning in place. The cultural cycle is an unending conversation between old people and young people, assuring the survival of local memory, which has, as long as it remains local, the greatest practical urgency and value. This is what is meant, and is all that is meant, by "sustainability". The fertility cycle turns by the law of nature. The cultural cycle turns on affection.

———

That we live now in an economy that is not sustainable is not the fault only of a few mongers of power and heavy equipment. We all are implicated. We all, in the course of our daily economic life, consent to it, whether or not we approve of it. This is because of the increasing abstraction and unconsciousness of our connection to our economic sources in the land, the land-communities, and the land-use economies. In my region and within my memory, for example, human life has become less creaturely and more engineered, less familiar and more remote from local places, pleasures, and associations. Our knowledge, in short, has become increasingly statistical.

Statistical knowledge once was rare. It was a property of the minds of great rulers, conquerors, and generals, people who succeeded or failed by the manipulation of large quantities that remained, to them, unimagined because unimaginable: merely accountable quantities of land, treasure, people, soldiers, and workers. This is the sort of knowledge we now call "data" or "facts" or "information". Or we call it "objective knowledge", supposedly untainted by personal attachment, but nonetheless available for industrial and commercial exploitation. By means of such knowledge a category assumes dominion over its parts or members. With the coming of industrialism, the great industrialists, like kings and conquerors, become exploiters of statistical knowledge. And finally virtually all of us, in order to participate and survive in their system, have had to agree to their substitution of statistical knowledge for personal knowledge. Virtually all of us now share with the most powerful industrialists their remoteness from actual experience of the actual world. Like them, we participate in an absentee economy, which makes us effectively absent even from our own dwelling places. Though most of us have little wealth and perhaps no power, we consumer-citizens are more like James B. Duke than we are like my grandfather. By economic proxies thoughtlessly given, by thoughtless consumption of goods ignorantly purchased, now we all are boomers.

———

The failure of imagination that divided the Duke monopoly and such farmers as my grandfather seems by now to be taken for granted. James B. Duke controlled remotely the economies of thousands of farm families. A hundred years later, "remote control" is an unquestioned fact, the realization of a technological ideal, and we have remote entertainment and remote war. Statistical knowledge is remote, and it isolates us in our remoteness. It is the stuff itself of unimagined life. We may, as we say, "know" statistical sums, but we cannot imagine them.

It is by imagination that knowledge is "carried to the heart" (to borrow again from Allen Tate) ("Ode to the Confederate Dead", *Collected Poems, 1919–1976*, 1989). The faculties of the mind — reason, memory, feeling, intuition, imagination, and the rest — are not distinct from one another. Though some may be favored over others and some ignored, none functions alone. But the human mind, even in its wholeness, even in instances of greatest genius, is irremediably limited. Its several faculties, when we try to use them separately or specialize them, are even more limited.

The fact is that we humans are not much to be trusted with what I am calling statistical knowledge, and the larger the statistical quantities the less we are to be trusted. We don't learn much from big numbers. We don't understand them very well, and we aren't much affected by them. The reality that is responsibly manageable by human intelligence is much nearer in scale to a small rural community or urban neighborhood than to the "globe".

When people succeed in profiting on a large scale, they succeed for themselves. When they fail, they fail for many others, sometimes for us all. A large failure is worse than a small one, and this has the sound of an axiom, but how many believe it? Propriety of scale in all human undertakings is paramount, and we ignore it. We are now betting our lives on quantities that far exceed all our powers of comprehension. We believe that we have built a perhaps limitless power of comprehension into computers and other machines, but our minds remain as limited as ever. Our trust that machines can manipulate to humane effect quantities that are unintelligible and unimaginable to humans is incorrigibly strange.

As there is a limit only within which property ownership is effective, so is there a limit only within which the human mind is effective and at least possibly beneficent. We must assume that the limit would vary somewhat, though not greatly, with the abilities of persons. Beyond that limit the mind loses its wholeness, and its faculties begin to be employed separately or fragmented according to the specialties or professions for which it has been trained.

———

In my reading of the historian John Lukacs, I have been most instructed by his understanding that there is no knowledge but human knowledge, that we are therefore inescapably central to our own consciousness, and that this is "a statement not of arrogance but of humility. It is yet another recognition of the inevitable limitations of mankind" (*Last Rites*, 2009). We are thus isolated within our uniquely human boundaries, which we certainly cannot transcend or escape by means of technological devices.

But as I understand this dilemma, we are not *completely* isolated. Though we cannot by our own powers escape our limits, we are subject to correction from, so to speak, the outside. I can hardly expect everybody to believe, as I do (with due caution), that inspiration can come from the outside. But inspiration is not the only way the human enclosure can be penetrated. Nature too may break in upon us, sometimes to our delight, sometimes to our dismay.

As many hunters, farmers, ecologists, and poets have understood, Nature (and here we capitalize her name) is the impartial mother of all creatures, unpredictable, never entirely revealed, not my mother or your mother, but nonetheless our mother. If we are observant and respectful of her, she gives good instruction. As Albert Howard, Wes Jackson, and others have carefully understood, she can give us the right patterns and standards for agriculture. If we ignore or offend her, she enforces her will with punishment. She is always trying to tell us that we are not so superior or independent or alone or autonomous as we may think. She tells us in the voice of Edmund Spenser that she is of *all* creatures "the equall mother, / And knittest each to each, as brother unto brother" (*The Faerie Queene*). Nearly three and a half centuries later, we hear her saying about the same thing in the voice of Aldo Leopold: "In short, a land ethic changes the role of *Homo sapiens* from conqueror of the land-community to plain member and citizen of it" (*A Sand County Almanac*).

We cannot know the whole truth, which belongs to God alone, but our task nevertheless is to seek to know what is true. And if we offend gravely enough against what we know to be true, as by failing badly enough to deal affectionately and responsibly with our land and our neighbors, truth will retaliate with ugliness, poverty, and disease. The crisis of this line of thought is the realization that we are at once limited and unendingly responsible for what we know and do.

———

The discrepancy between what modern humans presume to know and what they can imagine – given the background of pride and self-congratulation – is amusing and even funny. It becomes more serious as it raises issues of responsibility. It becomes fearfully serious when we start dealing with statistical measures of industrial destruction.

To hear of a thousand deaths in war is terrible, and we "know" that it is. But as it registers on our hearts, it is not more terrible than one death fully imagined. The economic hardship of one farm family, if they are our neighbors, affects us more painfully than pages of statistics on the decline of the farm population. I can be heartstruck by grief and a kind of compassion at the sight of one gulley (and by shame if I caused it myself), but, conservationist though I am, I am not nearly so upset by an accounting of the tons of plowland sediment borne by the Mississippi River. Wallace

Stevens wrote that "Imagination applied to the whole world is vapid in comparison to imagination applied to a detail" (*Opus Posthumous*, 1957) — and that appears to have the force of truth.

It is a horrible fact that we can read in the daily paper, without interrupting our breakfast, numerical reckonings of death and destruction that ought to break our hearts or scare us out of our wits. This brings us to an entirely practical question: can we — and, if we can, *how* can we — make actual in our minds the sometimes urgent things we say we know? This obviously cannot be accomplished by a technological breakthrough, nor can it be accomplished by a big thought. Perhaps it cannot be accomplished at all.

———

Yet another not very stretchable human limit is in our ability to tolerate or adapt to change. Change of course is a constant of earthly life. You can't step twice into exactly the same river, nor can you live two successive moments in exactly the same place. And always in human history there have been costly or catastrophic sudden changes. But with relentless fanfare, at the cost of almost indescribable ecological and social disorder, and to the almost incalculable enrichment and empowerment of corporations, industrialists have substituted what they fairly accurately call "revolution" for the slower, kinder processes of adaptation or evolution. We have had in only about two centuries a steady and ever-quickening sequence of industrial revolutions in manufacturing, transportation, war, agriculture, education, entertainment, homemaking and family life, health care, and so-called communications.

Probably everything that can be said in favor of all this has been said, and it is true that these revolutions have brought some increase of convenience and comfort and some easing of pain. It is also true that the industrialization of everything has incurred liabilities and is running deficits that have not been adequately accounted. All of these changes have depended upon industrial technologies, processes, and products, which have depended upon the fossil fuels, the production and consumption of which have been, and are still, unimaginably damaging to land, water, air, plants, animals, and humans. And the cycle of obsolescence and innovation, goaded by crazes of fashion, has given the corporate economy a controlling share of everybody's income.

The cost of this has been paid also in a social condition which apologists call "mobility", implying that it has been always "upward" to a "higher standard of living", but which in fact has been an ever-worsening unsettlement of our people, and the extinction or near-extinction of traditional and necessary communal structures.

For this also there is no technological or large-scale solution. Perhaps, as they believe, the most conscientiously up-to-date people can easily do without local workshops and stores, local journalism, a local newspaper, a local post office, all of which supposedly have been replaced by technologies. But what technology can replace personal privacy or the coherence of a family or a community? What technology can undo the collateral damages of an inhuman rate of technological change?

The losses and damages characteristic of our present economy cannot be stopped, let alone restored, by "liberal" or "conservative" tweakings of corporate industrialism, against which the ancient imperatives of good care, homemaking, and frugality can have no standing. The possibility of authentic correction comes, I think, from two already-evident causes. The first is scarcity and other serious problems arising from industrial abuses of the land-community. The goods of nature so far have been taken for granted and, especially in America, assumed to be limitless, but their diminishment, sooner or later unignorable, will enforce change.

A positive cause, still little noticed by high officials and the media, is the by now well-established effort to build or rebuild local economies, starting with economies of food. This effort to connect cities with their surrounding rural landscapes has the advantage of being both attractive and necessary. It rests exactly upon the recognition of human limits and the necessity of human scale. Its purpose, to the extent possible, is to bring producers and consumers, causes and effects, back within the bounds of neighborhood, which is to say the effective reach of imagination, sympathy, affection, and all else that neighborhood implies. An economy genuinely local and neighborly offers to localities a measure of security that they cannot derive from a national or a global economy controlled by people who, by principle, have no local commitment.

———

In this age so abstracted and bewildered by technological magnifications of power, people who stray beyond the limits of their mental competence typically find no guide except for the supposed authority of market price. "The market" thus assumes the standing of ultimate reality. But market value is an illusion, as is proven by its frequent changes; it is determined solely by the buyer's ability and willingness to pay.

By now our immense destructiveness has made clear that the actual value of some things exceeds human ability to calculate or measure, and therefore must be considered absolute. For the destruction of these things there is never, under any circumstances, any justification. Their absolute value is recognized by the mortal need of those who do not have them, and by affection. Land, to people who do not have it and who are thus without the means of life, is absolutely valuable. Ecological health, in a land dying of abuse, is not worth "something"; it is worth everything. And abused land relentlessly declines in value to its present and succeeding owners, whatever its market price.

But we need not wait, as we are doing, to be taught the absolute value of land and of land health by hunger and disease. Affection can teach us, and soon enough, if we grant appropriate standing to affection. For this we must look to the stickers, who "love the life they have made and the place they have made it in".

By now all thoughtful people have begun to feel our eligibility to be instructed by ecological disaster and mortal need. But we endangered ourselves first of all by dismissing affection as an honorable and necessary motive. Our decision in the middle of the last century to reduce the farm population, eliminating the allegedly "inefficient" small farmers, was enabled by the discounting of affection. As a result, we now have barely enough farmers to keep the land in production, with the help of increasingly expensive industrial technology and at an increasing ecological and social cost. Far from the plain citizens and members of the land-community, as Aldo Leopold wished them to be, farmers are now too likely to be merely the land's exploiters.

I don't hesitate to say that damage or destruction of the land-community is morally wrong, just as Leopold did not hesitate to say so when he was composing his essay, "The Land Ethic", in 1947. But I do not believe, as I think Leopold did not, that morality, even religious morality, is an adequate motive for good care of the land-community. The *primary* motive for good care and good use is always going to be affection, because affection involves us entirely. And here Leopold himself set the example. In 1935 he bought an exhausted Wisconsin farm and, with his family, began its restoration. To do this was morally right, of course, but the motive was affection. Leopold was an ecologist. He felt, we may be sure, an informed sorrow for the place in its ruin. He imagined it as it had been, as it was, and as it might be. And a profound, delighted affection radiates from every sentence he wrote about it.

Without this informed, practical, and *practiced* affection, the nation and its economy will conquer and destroy the country.

———

In thinking about the importance of affection, and of its increasing importance in our present world, I have been guided most directly by E.M. Forster's novel, *Howards End*, published in 1910. By then, Forster was aware of the implications of "rural decay" (*Howards End*), and in this novel he spoke, with some reason, of his fear that "the literature of the near future will probably ignore the country and seek inspiration from the town ... and those who care for the earth with sincerity may wait long ere the pendulum swings back to her again". Henry Wilcox, the novel's "plain man of business", speaks the customary rationalization, which has echoed through American bureaus and colleges of agriculture, almost without objection, for at least sixty years: "the days for small farms are over".

In *Howards End*, Forster saw the coming predominance of the machine and of mechanical thought, the consequent deracination and restlessness of populations, and the consequent ugliness. He saw an industrial ugliness, "a red rust", already creeping out from the cities into the countryside. He seems to have understood by then also that this ugliness was the result of the withdrawal of affection from places. To have beautiful buildings, for example, people obviously must want them to be beautiful and know how to make them beautiful, but evidently they also must love the places where the buildings are to be built. For a long time, in city and countryside, architecture has disregarded the nature and influence of places. Buildings have become as interchangeable from one place to another as automobiles. The outskirts of cities are virtually identical and as depressingly ugly as the corn-and-bean deserts of industrial agriculture.

What Forster could not have foreseen in 1910 was the *extent* of the ugliness to come. We still have not understood how far at fault has been the prevalent assumption that cities could be improved by pillage of the countryside. But urban life and rural life have now proved to be interdependent. As the countryside has become more toxic, more eroded, more ecologically degraded and more deserted, the cities have grown uglier, less sustainable, and less livable.

———

The argument of *Howards End* has its beginning in a manifesto against materialism:

> It is the vice of a vulgar mind to be thrilled by bigness, to think that a thousand square miles are a thousand times more wonderful than one square mile … That is not imagination. No, it kills it. … Your universities? Oh, yes, you have learned men who collect … facts, and facts, and empires of facts. But which of them will rekindle the light within?

"The light within", I think, means affection, affection as motive and guide. Knowledge without affection leads us astray every time. Affection leads, by way of good work, to authentic hope. The factual knowledge, in which we seem more and more to be placing our trust, leads only to hope of the discovery, endlessly deferrable, of an ultimate fact or smallest particle that at last will explain everything.

The climactic scene of Forster's novel is the confrontation between its heroine, Margaret Schlegel, and her husband, the self-described "plain man of business", Henry Wilcox. The issue is Henry's determination to deal, as he thinks, "realistically" with a situation that calls for imagination, for affection, and then forgiveness. Margaret feels at the start of their confrontation that she is "fighting for women against men". But she is not a feminist in the popular or political sense. What she opposes with all her might is Henry's hardness of mind and heart that is "realistic" only because it is expedient and because it subtracts from reality the life of imagination and affection, of living souls. She opposes his refusal to see the practicality of the life of the soul.

Margaret's premise, as she puts it to Henry, is the balance point of the book: "It all turns on affection now … Affection. Don't you see?"

In a speech delivered in 2006, "Revitalizing Rural Communities", Frederick Kirschenmann quoted his friend Constance Falk, an economist:

"There is a new vision emerging demonstrating how we can solve problems and at the same time create a better world, and it all depends on collaboration, love, respect, beauty, and fairness" (*In Cultivating an Ecological Conscience*, 2011).

Those two women, almost a century apart, speak for human wholeness against fragmentation, disorder, and heartbreak. The English philosopher and geometer Keith Critchlow brings his own light to the same point: "The human mind takes apart with its analytic habits of reasoning but the human heart puts things together because it loves them …" (*The Hidden Geometry of Flowers*, 2011).

—

The great reassurance of Forster's novel is the wholeheartedness of his language. It is to begin with a language not disturbed by mystery, by things unseen. But Forster's interest throughout is in soul-sustaining habitations: houses, households, earthly places where lives can be made and loved. In defense of such dwellings he uses, without irony or apology, the vocabulary that I have depended on in this talk: truth, nature, imagination, affection, love, hope, beauty, joy. Those words are hard to keep still within definitions; they make the dictionary hum like a beehive. But in such words, in their resonance within their histories and in their associations with one another, we find our indispensable humanity, without which we are lost and in danger.

No doubt there always will be some people willing to do anything at all that is economically or technologically possible, who look upon the world and its creatures without affection and therefore as exploitable without limit. Against that limitlessness, in which we foresee assuredly our ruin, we have only our ancient effort to define ourselves as human and humane. But this ages-long, imperfect, unendable attempt, with its magnificent record, we have virtually disowned by assigning it to the ever more subordinate set of school subjects we call "arts and humanities" or, for short, "culture". Culture, so isolated, is seen either as a dead-end academic profession or as a mainly useless acquisition to be displayed and appreciated "for its own sake". This definition of culture as "high culture" actually debases it, as it debases also the presumably low culture that is excluded: the arts, for example, of land use, life support, healing, housekeeping, homemaking.

I don't like to deal in categorical approvals, and certainly not of the arts. Even so, I do not concede that the "fine arts", in general, are useless or unnecessary or even impractical. I can testify that some works of art, by the usual classification fine, have instructed, sustained, and comforted me for many years in my opposition to industrial pillage.

But I would insist that the economic arts are just as honorably and authentically refinable as the fine arts. And so I am nominating economy for an equal standing among the arts and humanities. I mean, not economics, but economy, the making of the human household upon the earth: the *arts of adapting kindly* the many human households to the earth's many ecosystems and human neighborhoods. This is the economy that the most public and influential economists never talk about, the economy that is the primary vocation and responsibility of every one of us.

———

My grandparents were fortunate. They survived their debts and kept their farm – finally, and almost too late, with help from my father, who had begun his law practice in the county seat. But in the century and more since that hard year of 1907, millions of others have not been so fortunate. Owing largely to economic constraints, they have lost their hold on the land, and the land has lost its hold on them. They have entered into the trial of displacement and scattering that we try to dignify as "mobility".

Even so, land and people have suffered together, as invariably they must. Under the rule of industrial economics, the land, our country, has been pillaged for the enrichment, supposedly, of those humans who have claimed the right to own or exploit it without limit. Of the land-community much has been consumed, much has been wasted, almost nothing has flourished.

But this has not been inevitable. We do not have to live as if we are alone.

This essay was the 2012 Jefferson Lecture, delivered on 23 April, 2012, at the Kennedy Center for the Performing Arts, in Washington, DC.

A poet, fiction-writer, essayist, cultural critic, activist and farmer, as well as one of America's foremost public intellectuals, Wendell Berry was born in 1934, in Port Royal, Kentucky. He is the author of 30 volumes of non-fiction, 15 works of fiction, and 26 books of poetry. His latest publication is A Place in Time *(Counterpoint, 2012), a collection of short stories. He continues to live in Port Royal, where his family has farmed for five generations.*

POEM

Aidan Rooney

RECOLLECTION

> *Ramassez donc vos pêches*
> (*Les Pêches*, André Theuriet)

I met him just the once astride his horse,
looking for all the world the part of Lord.
A pack of hounds a fox had driven hoarse
wove beneath his boots a natural guard,
straying only to nose among the gorse.
I was headed home from his orchard,
at the one point in a stream I could cross,
apples slung in the gut of my tee-shirt.

Decades later, one of those teaching lulls
when a text will exact reminiscence.
A fine day, young man, for picking apples.
I felt my blood rise, the ring of my silence
as his dogs plashed around me where I stood
on a wobbly stone. And the Lord rode onward.

Aidan Rooney was born in Monaghan in 1965 and educated at St Patrick's College, Maynooth. He is the author of two collections of poems, Day Release *(2000) and* Tightrope *(2007), both from The Gallery Press. Since 1988, he has taught French and English at Thayer Academy, Massachusetts.*

THE VIEW FROM THE GLEN

Cathal Ó Searcaigh

After India.

We overlook the wonders that surround us, the neighbouring worlds of nature.

Birds, beasts, plant life, the mineral domain, they are also our close kin who share the same earth with us. We are as much animal, vegetable, mineral as we are human. We are all carbon kindred, an intermingling family of the same stock element. It's a lineage that binds all living matter inasmuch as blood binds kith and kin.

We are in our element, so to say, when we align ourselves to their familiar presences, to their energies. You are never alone when you acknowledge and appreciate the presence of these intimates. I know that for some the angst of being alone and apart is indeed very real – a deep-seated lonesomeness, arising from a firm belief that we are all separate entities. I lean towards the idea of shared origins, a familiar carbon ethnicity that binds us and yet lets us be boundless.

On my daily walks around the glen I open up and enjoy the spirited communion of being a participant in this vibrant world. I'm ceaselessly surprised by the wild diversity flourishing around me. And I'm constantly being lifted, emotionally and imaginatively, beyond my own enclosed life into the life of all, into immense existence.

What sights and what sounds? I will see a higgledy parade of thistles by the wayside or, maybe, a nervy rabbit crouching in the rushes. A far-off farm lit up in a splash of light – or a red dangle of fuchsia – will brighten my way.

I'll tingle with joy at a white glissade of swans on Loch an Ghainimh. I will breathe in the honeysuckle's sweet exhalation in Caiseal na gCorr. I'll marvel at the collusions of sunset colours above Carn Traona, a grand wreckage of amber and violet, ivory and gold, ochre and oyster, blazing across the sky.

I will be close to the click and tap of a wren in a dry-stone wall and to a robin with its little song aquiver in the winter twigs. I will be alert to buds greening on a spring branch, and to a quartz rock resplendent on a sunny hillside.

I will greet the leafy tongue of grasses; respond to the grope of roots, to the sharp bristle of a briar, to the abrupt stir of a moorhen, to a mousy bat foraging in the dark.

I will find peace at the Dúloch, watching a Milky Way of water-lilies stretching across the stellar silence of its waters. And I will attend to my own salvation, not by submitting to the words and beliefs of others but by attuning myself to the deep humming of bees in the flowering heather of Mín a' Leá; to the fraternity of mosses at Páirc Mheabha; to the hawthorn on Andy's Farm, a profligate of joy, bridal-white in summer, berry-red in winter; to the chant of wind across the acres of wild bog in Altan; to rainlight, to cloudswirls, to sunspots.

Seeing the forthright authority of a lone ash-tree, the spontaneity of daisies and the patience and resolve of a bog asphodel, I will feel blessed to be a part of this planetary community, this largeness of life.

I know that if I act in consonance with it I will always have this bountiful experience. And I will live generously.

———

Be a devotee of yourself. Allow a truly alive spirituality to rise up from within your own intuitive depths instead of clinging to some moribund code of beliefs imposed upon you.

Spirituality should be a joyful inward journey, a happy communion between head and heart.

Spirituality is about how you behave, how you befriend, how you cope with anguish, with anecdotes, with anger; how you bear up and endure and come through.

It's not about a strict adherence to ritual and liturgy. It's not about self-denial and an abandoning of the appetites. It's not about a dependence on theological doctrines and a passive acceptance of moral populism.

A truly spiritual life is a fulfilled life where your own unique potential, your positive expression of living, shines forth to brighten and better the world.

You will know a spiritual person by the ease with which he deals with himself and the natural grace with which he deals with others.

———

Come to know the space you inhabit, where your arms are, your head, your feet. Standing upright, your feet firmly on the ground, your head aloft, centre yourself within this space.

Take in the stretch and spread of your limbs. Explore this space, get your bearings within it, familiarize yourself with its limits, its boundaries. Know its reach and range. Understand that you are accountable for it.

From within this complex of space, you move, breathe, act, speak. Recognize the actuality of that. Occupy it with care. It's your sacred indwelling.

Learn to govern yourself well within this space. After all, you are responsible for its interactions with others.

Be strong without being stubborn. Be assertive without being aggressive. Be challenging without being contrary. Be still without being sullen.

Revere your own space and you will, as a matter of course, respect the space of others. You will know how to place your own fragile space beside someone else's equally fragile space, gently and graciously.

You will heed the needs of others, showing a gracious sensitivity to all sentient beings in their respective spaces. This is what loving your neighbour truly means – to accommodate with decency, to acknowledge with dignity, all those who co-exist with you.

Cathal Ó Searcaigh is the Irish Language Editor of this journal. He was born in 1956 and raised in Meenala, near Gortahork, an Irish-speaking district in Co Donegal. His poetry collections are Súile Shuibhne *(Coiscéim, 1983),* Suibhne *(Coiscéim, 1987), the bilingual* An Bealach 'na Bhaile/Homecoming *(Cló Iar-Chonnachta, 1993),* Ag Tnúth Leis an tSolas *(Cló Iar-Chonnachta, 1993),* Na Buachaillí Bána *(Cló Iar-Chonnachta, 1996), the selected* Out in the Open *(Cló Iar-Chonnachta, 2000),* Gúrú i gCluídíní *(2006),* An tAm Marfach ina Mairimid *(2011), and* Aimsir Ársa *(2013). His prose works include* Seal i Neipeal *(2004),* Light on Distant Hills: A Memoir *(2009), and* Pianó Mhín na bPreáchán *(2011). He is also the author several plays in Irish, and a selection of English translations of his poetry,* By the Hearth at Mín a' Leá *(Arc), appeared in 2005. He continues to live in Meenala, and is a member of Aosdána.*

DÁN

Paddy Bushe

DO AONGHAS ÚRGHLAS AG 70

So what má tá an dubh curtha go snasta ina gheal ort
Ag an aimsir? Ní raibh dul amú ort riamh faoi ghile

Nó dorchadas na cruinne, agus níor nós leat taobhú
Le dearcadh dubh-is-bán na súl géar úd atá dall

Ar an gcrotal glasuaithne i léithe na carraige,
Dall ar mhaostacht ildaite gach ní inár dtimpeall,

Agus bodhar ar iliomadúileacht leagan an scéil
Atá á chanadh gan tús gan deireadh ar fud na cruinne.

A Aonghais Dhuibh, a Aonghais Ghil, a ghlaise úir:
Lean ort ag boilgearnach thar maoil na dteorainneacha uile.

Nár ruga riamh ceartchreideamhacht ort, is nár thaga ort
Mór-is-fiú na gceannlitreacha nó saoithíneacht na lánstad.

FOR EVERGREEN AONGHAS AT 70

So what if time has fooled you, and turned the dark hair
White? You've never been deluded about the brightness

Or darkness of the world. But you've never given in
To the black and white view, to those who are blind

To the viridescent lichen in the greyness of the rock,
Blind to the multi-coloured saturation of everything around us,

And deaf to the myriad versions of the story constantly
Sung without beginning or ending all over the world.

Aonghas Dubh. Aonghas Bán. Green-reflecting wellspring:
Don't ever stop bubbling over the brim of all the boundaries.

May orthodoxy never overtake you, may you never suffer
The self-importance of the capital, the pedantry of the full stop.

See p. 45 for four poems in Scots by Aonghas MacNeacail.

Paddy Bushe was born in Dublin in 1948, and now lives in Waterville, Co Kerry. He writes in both Irish and English, and has published eight collections of poetry, most recently To Ring in Silence: New and Selected Poems *(Dedalus, 2008), a bilingual volume.*

TRÍ DHÁN

Mícheál Ó Ruairc

AR AN TRAEIN GO CABRACH

Dailc bheag de chailín scoile
in éide de ghlas na gcaorach
tráthnóna caoch geimhridh
nach gcuirfeá do bhrocaire draoibe amach
i do sheasamh go diongbháilte
i lár an phasáiste chaoil
ar an traein ó Stáisiún na bPiarsach
go Cabrach gur cuma sa tsioc
leat a bhfuil timpeall ort
a bheith ann nó as is tú ag freagairt
do ghutháin phóca i nGaeilge
neamhghlan Ghaelscoile
in ard do chinn is do ghutha
beag beann ar sracfhéachaintí
doicheallacha agus ar dhreachanna
díchreidmheacha do chomhphaisinéirí
mo ghraidhin go deo thú
a chailín bhig na teanga binne
nach dtugann cúl le cine
ag spalpadh leat i dteanga do chroí
's tú mo Ghráinne Mhaol mo Róisín Dubh
mo Dhroimeann Donn Dílis
mo Réaltann na Spéirchoinneal gCaomh
ar do bhealach abhaile ón scoil
ar an traein go Cabrach
ar thráthnóna caoch geimhreidh
nach gcuirfeá do bhrocaire draoibe amach

FUAIMEANNA

Sa chiúnas a lean an argóint
a bhí eadrainn
an oíche sin
d'éisteamar leis na tonnta
ag briseadh ar an trá
i bhfad uainn
agus d'fhéadfaimis fear a chloisint
ag gnúsacht
bean ag éagaoin
spriongaí leapa ag gíoscán
ar mire
i seomra codlata éigin
a bhí trasna an dorchla
uainn
san óstán beag
2-réalta

STRACADH

"Love Will Tear Us Apart"
an t-amhrán a bhí á chasadh
ar an *jukebox*
an oíche úd i gCorcaigh
an cuimhin leat?

Agus dhein.
Mar a stracfadh conairt
chraosach con
giorria sceimhlithe
as a chéile
stracadh óna chéile sinn
is gan an bheirt
againn
ach ar thús cadhnaíochta
ár gcumainn.

Mícheál Ó Ruairc was born in 1953 in Brandon, Cloghane, in the West Kerry Gaeltacht of An Leitriúch, on the Dingle Peninsula. He received a BA degree from University College Cork in 1974, and a MA in Modern Irish from St Patrick's College Maynooth in 1991. He is the author of three collections of poetry, one volume of short stories and twelve novels in Irish, as well as one book of poems in English, Humane Killing *(Aisling Press, 1992). He recently retired from teaching, and now resides in Dublin.*

DÁN

Dairena Ní Chinnéide

AN LÁ A BHUAILEAS LE BÚDA I MÍN A' LEÁ

do Chathal Ó Searcaigh

Bhuaileas le Búda i Mín a' Leá
tráthnóna samhraidh.

Bhí Matisse i bhfochair beirt bhan
i mbun ranga sa leithreas,
is ceathrar dineasár
caite go cóireach
ar imeall an fholcadáin,
ar nós turasóirí
ó chian ársa.

Bhíodar ciúin, dea-mhúinte,
ach, ní raibh aon tuairm acu
cad a bhí á rá
ag na spéirmhnáibh ar an bhfalla,
gnúsachtaíl an t-aon teanga
a labharadar 'ge baile.

Tré dhearúd éigin maorfhlaithiúil,
zappáileadh na bocanna
is na girseacha réamh-dhaonna seo
trén scoilt idir chruinne
is réaltbhuíon na samhlaíochta.

Tar éis a dturas idir-ghalactach
leandáileadar ag doras
draoi-bhúda, in aprún bándearg,
a thuig a mbriathra
i dteanga na daonnachta
a labhair a chroí
le friotal na féile.

I gcúirt an draoi
tá fráma ar phictúirí do mhian,
is mianach na fáilte, crochta
in iarsmalann an áthais.

Laismuigh, i bhfiacail sléibhe
seinntear ceol
cumtha le marmar bán an bhráithreachais
is éabhar cruaidh na tuisceana.

Ceol múnlaithe as meas
ar chine gach crann
is ginealach na ngabhar
i mbriathra gan breithiúnas.

Thóg mo chroí stóinséaratha
sliocht as leabhar na gcnoc
is teilgeadh mé
go tearmann tláth an áthais.

Ansan de gheit,
d'eitil meitheal peidhleacáin
as réiltíní m-anama
ag claochlú i gcéilí mo choinsias.

Thuigeas láithreach
go raibh mná Mhatisse
ag teagasc Gaelic Thír Chonaill
do dhíneasáir an fholcadáin.

Ba bhundúchasaigh sinn
as treabh caoin an Uile
ag canadh iomann ár gcroíthe istigh

an lá a bhuaileas le Búda i Mín a' Leá
tráthnóna samhraidh!

A playwright and script-writer as well as a poet, Dairena Ní Chinnéide lives in Ballyferriter, on the Dingle Peninsula, Co Kerry, where she was born in 1969. She holds a degree in Communications Studies from Dublin City University and a Higher Diploma in Translation Studies from University College, Galway. She is the author of five collections of poems, most recently Bleachtaire na Seirce *(Coiscéim, 2010). She is currently working on Irish-language versions of a selection of poems by the Russian poet Marina Tsvetaeva, and has completed a new bilingual collection,* Rí Rá.

DHÁ DHÁN

Stiofán Ó Díreáin

ALZHEIMER'S

"Cé thusa?"

"Nach cuimhin leat aghaidh d'iníne?
Nach n-aithníonn tú céad toradh do bhroinne?"

"Cé thusa?"
"Cá bhfuil tú, a Mhamaí?"

Chuardaigh mé í
Fríd rosca fliucha
Agus í ag déanamh slabhra nóiníní
I léana a hóige,
Nó ag dul amach is isteach fríd na cloigíní gorma
I gclós na scoile,
Nó ag caitheamh bláthfhleisce
Ar lá a pósta,
Nó ag fíodóireacht lín
Ar sheolta cíocracha,
Nó ag síorsclábhaíocht
Ag umar na cistine,
Nó ag spraoiscreadaíl in ard a gutha
Ar uair mo bhreithe.

Ag smaoineamh dom
Ar cheo i do shúile,
Ar rámhaillí do bhaothchainte,
Ar laige do chnámh cráite,
Is tú bean bhláfar m'óige
Is mé ag teacht ar mo chéill,
Is tú seanchailleach scólach i ndeireadh na déithe
Is tú ag coraíocht le do chéill.

"Tá tú amuigh leis na féileacáin, a Mhamaí,
Ach ní fheicim aon phúdar beannaithe.
Is síogaí thú, d'anam goidte.
Ach an le Dia nó le Diabhal thú?"

SPEABHRAÍDÍ

Arna aistriú ag Stiofán Ó Direáin dán a scríobh Aonghus Dubh MacNeacail

Chuaigh mé inné go dtí an chollchoill
Ar thóir cnónna fá choinne bí
Ach ní fhaca mé ach d'éadan
Mar chathú ar gach craobh.
Chuaigh mé inné go trá an chnuasaigh
Lón de ruacáin a bhaint
Nocht a huile bhlaosc péarla
D'áilleachtsa a lua.

Chuaigh mé isteach i dteach an leanna
Le tú a dhíbirt as mo cheann;
Le gach gloine a shlog mé steall do
Mhaise as go teann.
Chuaigh mé go luath chun na leapa
Le tú a ruaigeadh le suan,
Ach ní thabharfá cead dom codladh
Nó go ndéanfainn duan.

D'iarrfainn bheith saor ó do thóraíocht
Ach bheadh muid scartha ónár gcéill:
Do chuma a bheith in áit do shamhla,
Bheadh an-lúcháir orm.
D'fhág tú mé mar bhómán baoth
Mo chairde á mbodhrú le do chlú;
Má thig tú tchífidh siad nach bhfuil
Mearú orm fiú.

Tchífidh siad binn is marbhshruth,
Dallán is iolar insa ríl,
Feamainn go caomh ar altram sú
Ag suirí faoina súile.
Tchífidh siad mis' is tusa ag súgradh
Gob ar ghob, mar anáil amháin:
Ag muirniú mar seo de shíor, le
Chéile go raibh ár maoin.

Stiofán Ó Díreáin was born in Belfast in 1947, and took degrees in physics from Queen's University Belfast and Imperial College London, before working many years in the power industry in England. His poems and short stories have appeared in a number of Irish-language journals. Now retired, he lives in Millbay, Islandmagee, Co Antrim.

SEVENTEEN GENERATIONS

Michelle O Riordan

On this island, in this century.

In *A Twisted Root: Ancestral Entanglements in Ireland* (Blackstaff Press, 2012), Patricia Craig has chosen to share her genealogical history with us, to expose her family tree to some brief scrutiny and to let us consider the hinterland of a person of her name, age, station and occupation – and of her opinions and political, social and religious affiliations.

The narrative covers a period of some four and a half centuries: about 17 generations of people who are on record as having lived, worked, loved, been loved and died on this 70,000-odd square kilometres of land and fresh water – the island of Ireland. And every inch of this existence is a matter of contest, and controversy. Each kilometre and every breath is one which no one can take for granted.

Craig follows the life and times of these 17 generations in a superbly imaginative engagement with history. She projects real people onto the known narrative of what we call history, the sketchy and half-realizable tracks which we use as mental maps to our past, our present and our future.

Our familiarity with the framing narrative, of whatever tradition, is the merest cryptic nod to events that had real actors, real dilemmas and concrete results. It is the great triumph of this book that Patricia Craig gives us a family upon which to hang the frame. A family that in all its extraordinary ramifications engages us on a personal level with events for which we have great feeling but almost no understanding.

Tracking traceable names through various and multifarious records of every available kind, Craig allows the tenor of the sources to dictate the narrative of the time. The early pioneering zeal of her earliest (traceable) English settler forbears; the new-world quality of their settlement in the town of Lisnagarvey/Lisburn; the terror and horror of the war that broke out in a tumult of violence in 1641; the varieties of allegiance that characterized the Loyalist, the Briton and the Irish in the war of the three kings; the trimming and compromise that followed the clear victory and defeat that opened into the eighteenth century; the courage and intrepidity of the young German woman who made her life in nineteenth-century

Dublin, and the stalwart father whose sense of family solidarity overcame his sense of denominational solidarity.

The book traces the laying down of cultural tracks that left later generations with constricted choices of movement and of allegiance, and the characteristic kicking over of those traces that occurs in vital families every couple of generations, leading us into the activism of the later centuries and right down to the most recent hotly contested past. Religion and politics and economics and social life, cultural life, farming, trading, the services and service itself down through the generations are made real for us in characters and families with whom we become familiar, and indeed in whose careers and marriages and families and landholdings and scrapes with the law, and political allegiances, we find ourselves ever more involved.

I had my personal favourites – the prudent James Tipping, who died in dignity in 1853 unlike his improvident brother; the clear-headed bigoted William Blacker, whose clarity had its own integrity. Others will latch on to their own favourites and follow the sedate Letts in Wexford and their horrible experiences during the 1798 rebellion; others still will head for 1920 and go with the "bicycle men" and women on their clandestine missions participating in yet another momentous historical period.

Temporally, the book occupies about four different time zones: the time at which you yourself are reading it (and all the ambient noise of that time – radio, internet, iPod and so forth); the time the author is presenting in the main focus of the tale of her progenitors (1670, 1770, 1970 and so on); the time to which she refers during these discourses – a time which ranges back and forth over books read, poems remembered, snatches of song encapsulating a feeling, a moment or a mood, and the remembered reminiscences of a loved interlocutor, mother, father or cousin. The fourth temporal world in this book is the timeless zone of narrative, history, memory, creation and representation.

The rich palimpsest of this zoneless time, place and cause of writing is a multi-textured, dense and hugely satisfying realization of an impossible task. It is the dream achievement of the individual who knows that his/her roots go back to Adam, but who has no idea how that might work out; it is a fleshed-out genealogical tree that is the individual story of the author, but to which we can each tie a little rag, or a little ribbon. We know that the same goes for all of us.

The story is a story of commitment, loyalty and steadfastness, in the first instance to family, and from there to village, town, and province – a commitment to peace, prosperity and progress and a willingness on all sides to risk all to preserve the shape of the family held in the heart and held in the head. Its huge sweep makes real the honourable, charitable and well-meaning effort of the majority of humankind to make an honest living among honest people for the good of all.

Action in defence of these values does not always make this fundamental forward and decent trajectory of the actors immediately clear or likeable: the kind of commitment that might well appear in history as a great communal conflagration, a violent tear across a century, a long-standing open wound. And yet, Craig's book assures us that the majority tendency to harmony, hybridity and humour usually carries the everyday with it, and makes the episodic outbursts painful but surmountable at the same time.

The various ways and means and motives that shaped this commitment and the variety of expressions it took is the actual stuff of this enormous family saga. It is a saga that takes us from sixteenth-century England to sixteenth-century Ireland and kicks off the great adventure of 17 generations that brings us to this day in this place and this author.

The very qualities that allowed Patricia Craig to catch a thread of her ancestors right down the almost five centuries are those same that drove her ancestors to be active participants in the story of their country, and gave her the energy and courage to examine them in all their variety, to accept them in all their positive and negative qualities, and to own her place on this island in this century. Ownership and acceptance of variegation and hybridity are the underlying currents in this work; pride, humour and integrity are the overt qualities that make it a thoroughly enchanting read, and a total entrapment for several hours of absorption with Ireland in every aspect of its existence – and thereby with the essence of the human condition.

What else are great books for?

The above address was given at the launch of A Twisted Root *on 16 October 2012 at Clifton House, Belfast.*

Michelle O Riordan is Assistant Professor for Publications at the School of Celtic Studies, Dublin Institute for Advanced Studies. She is the author of The Gaelic Mind and the Collapse of the Gaelic World *(1990) and* Irish Bardic Poetry and Rhetorical Reality *(2007), both from Cork University Press.*

IN OTHER WORDS: FROM THE QUÉBÉCOIS

A HEARTH FOR MY HEART
from i^2

Gilles Pellerin

Time, that beautiful country.

EVERYONE SANG LIKE A BARITONE

Everyone sang like a baritone. Men and women changed. All became radicals. Here, there, they lit wastefires, picketfires, bonfires. They were celebrating not the enemy's loss, but their own victory. All night long, they would remain pure. For the rest of their lives they would remember this moment as the time they were pure.

As I made my way back to the hotel, I crossed paths with a party of men and women intoning at the top of their voices, each one a baritone for the occasion.

I understood why youth could be a bother to some, remembering those colleagues who did not care one bit for enthusiasm, confidence, faith and the future. I was sad for being old enough to realize that youth is what came to others, and to the young; my wood was dry and gray.

Yet my heart beat with joy, and I grew tipsy for being younger than the age of despair.

SARTRE

Some days Jean-Paul Sartre with his usual slow stride finds his way back to Paris, not too far from the crossroads where he used to play in the role of the pedlar in *The People's Cause*. He is standing where he is now standing, with his new eye someone made for him. When they popped a mirror to his face, he became giddy about his own good looks. He asked if whether they would dye his hair in a lighter colour. It would make him ten, one hundred years younger.

He avoids going to the cafés he used to frequent. Still, he can't escape the Rive Gauche, where he idles in front of the bookstands just as their owners call it a day. He hopes to find a closing-time deal and surreptitiously inspects the price tag on his own books. His share price is on the wane. Boxes are tapped shut and marked with tags. What would I give to know what he thinks of his works, but such thoughts he keeps to himself. A woman managing a bookstand recognizes the professional *flâneur* Sartre is, just like she likes them. She nods to him as he walks away homeward-bound, following his cane, in the sunset. I never found the courage to follow him home, out of politeness, and surely out of respect.

One day I noticed him in a park, sitting in the shadows, the skin of a man who goes to bed early. He was unaware of the elderly woman, wobbly on her legs, walking towards him, eyeing the empty spot on the bench which Sartre secured for himself, more precious than any bench at the French Academy.

This afternoon, I caught him staring with that look of his, talking with the woman bookseller. They held a canon of sorts, sparkle in their eyes. He seemed to have aged, he was ten years, one hundred years older than the man who unrepentantly came on to girls who could have been his granddaughters. There, a young man, lit up like in a film-set, a young woman and an older man. Recently arrived, fiery, all fresh, he was a man of morals and desire, coveting the woman. So what if to get his catch he must start reading books again. Sartre recognized the faces made by the model, which he has already dealt with. For a second, he told himself that the past is out of reach, and that the days of seduction are long gone. The bookseller, she did not agree. So he kept her to himself.

———

SUCH IS NOW

It is early, so early that no one has yet left his mark on the snow-covered sidewalk. My bones are not quite awake. Around my knees, the bitter bow of time resounds. Then, nothing. I try to concentrate on the mechanics of walking. To which speechlessness alone can respond. My feet sink deep in the silent concert of matter become taciturn. First of white mornings, downtown.

I am not totally saying the truth. People are coming and going behind the doors of their homes. Cars rush by. Between its smoker's coughs, the city grasps for air. My ears can barely absorb it all, too dizzy are they with the noise my footsteps should be producing but are not.

Bliss in such precision can never last. Snow begins to fall. Too much snow, my soles are making the sound of someone chewing. My footsteps and I find ourselves alone. I am waiting for a thought that won't rise, which would be welcomed by the innocence of the sidewalk. No such luck. I exist outside the metaphysical world, far from metaphors, far from even the most obvious of metaphors. Before me, harmony. Behind me, my footsteps revealed, duck's-feet mackle. In between, there is the morning. Time balancing, time opening up to my childhood days when, boots deep in the fresh-fallen snow, I found the meaning of being solemn. And then, at a different time, a second childhood rises, my children waking before daybreak, they are ready to taste the nobility of the world. Such is now.

I am ageless when I walk. The factories of time have yet to open their gates.

———

ALL RED

What strikes them first is the profusion of colours. Anyone who visits the Laurentians at the beginning of October, before the stormy winds and cold rain, anyone who stays at Portneuf understands right away. Yes, we are embraced by a sense of fulfilment, the light glorious everywhere, the landscape boasting its magnificence, the forest balancing on what could be called silence. A pause. Such calmness surprises in the delirium of colours. Gold is what most of the world shares. Everyone should be screaming, trees, kings gone mad in the centre of their wealth. Midas, Croesus, Louis XIV, Rockefeller.

They might come from distant lands, yet they all fall silent here as they would in the Louvre. We begin to chatter as in a chorus, laughing, exclaiming in unison. My friend, Michel, met back in the sixteenth century, explains the difference between "profusion of colours" and "profusion in colour". With his hands he traces the borderline that divides the red, all the red, and us. Everything in me exudes American pride. Still, something lies beyond me. "Still, something lies beyond me."

"Gilles, what about friendship?" Neither the oldest mountains in the world nor my friends need to repay back the favour. Friends wanted to visit the country site, and the most beautiful country in the world opened up to them.

A month later, beauty multiplies. Streams blotted by rain offer new interpretations of time. Water knows only black and white. Cold, depth, chaos, fog on treetops, and beyond mountains … Now the Batiscan River is impatient, impetuous, she knows ice is soon to come. The landscape blends with the colour of the running stream: black and white. Here, there, the road we take intersects with the path of the forest on which might appear, and to no one's surprise, a hunter, rifle bent under his arm, and in his hand a bundle of partridges tied by their feet. I remember European autumns, and wonder which is romantic – the colour or the lack of colour. I have no doubt a reply will now arise. From Europe I move on to thinking of my friends. Marie tells me that she is thinking about them as well, and I am not at all surprised. We begin to talk of Anaïs, Thiery, Jamel, Michel. Even at a distance, friendship is a hearth.

We step out of the car. The air is frigid, saturated, humid. This is the way the universe seeps deep into us. Make sure you wrap your scarf around your neck. Hers is red, the only visible colour on this canvas. The conversation turns to Paul, about what he had to say on poetry. His words enhance the joy of the present moment: poetry changes the landscape into a blanket we pull within. We step back into silence, become the landscape. Together. Her cheeks are now a colour calling out to my lips.

—

THE KINGS

The project appeared to me one afternoon when it became clear that the cold would persist and the rain which had fallen the night before would in the morning become a pool of ice hard enough for the children to skate on. Though asphalt surrounded the house, construction works during that winter prevented us from using the space as a parking lot.

Hence my project. What about a skating rink? By passing water-filled pails through the washroom window we could easily spread the water over the snow. This was the first year since moving to our house in which the climate seemed perfect for a rink. On 6 January, snow had gathered on the space that separated our house from the neighbours. The cold was just right before turning unbearable, hard ice can rapidly change into strips of flaky snow, and heaps of frazil ice is never good for what I wanted to do.

I handed Ariane the first pail, which she dropped as she slipped, legs flying above her head, her snowsuit covered with water and ice. When I exclaimed that my idea was really stupid, she argued: "Daddy, oh no. It was a brilliant idea." Her younger brother Antoine chanted in agreement. And so we started all over again. The assembly line began: sink, window, rink. With no mention of ground, parking lot, asphalt. The moment, a noble adventure. We busied ourselves till sunset. And when Agathe returned home, she was as enthusiastic as her younger siblings. "Keep the assembly line going, and I'll bake an Epiphany cake."

The winter semester had started, and it kept snowing. The skating rink was holding firm. The children would skate after school, no matter how frigid the cold was. We played hockey, they with skates, I in my boots. ("Antoine, my weight will break the ice.") When I came back after a day's work, I'd fixed the ice by rubbing water and snow on the cracks. The side board rose higher and higher, while the rink grew narrower and narrower after each snowfall. We shovelled the snow, Ariane behind a plank of plywood against which I pushed the snow. Antoine's job consisted of stamping the snow with his feet, acting like the "foreman" (to quote my mother). My back did not complain for an entire month, but then a snowstorm of 30 centimetres broke me.

That night we invited friends to supper. Agathe had baked her Epiphany cake, which we placed in such a way that the youngest child, Jérémie, this time around, would find the pea in his slice. We have been cheating in our family for generations, making sure the youngest would always be the fortunate king of the party. Jérémie was unaware of custom. Few families celebrate the Epiphany. And we ourselves rarely do. Antoine had become old enough to skip over the tantrum of not being king, and Ariane old enough to fashion a crown with cardboard cut from boxes on which she drew yellow and red abstract figures.

Luck sometimes needs assistance for it not to go berserk. One of our children had accidentally pushed the plate destined to Jérémie to me, but we hadn't enough time to fix the error. We had asked the children to be alert and careful, but the advice should have been directed to me. When I bit into the cake with some force, I almost cracked my tooth on the pea.

Everyone was shocked, and every child had noticed what had happened. Still Ariane put the crown on my head and, so for a couple of minutes, I became king of the world. All applauded. But I had to abdicate and I passed the precious crown on to Jeremy I. "Long Live the King!"

Of all the reigns, Gilles the Shortlived was the happiest.

———

AUTUMN'S STORIES

Not far from the house I grew up in was a cornfield. A small forest led down to the river which flowed on both sides of the Saint-Maurice. Friends from distant countries claim that this place is the land of the autumn season. My father, whose family had settled the region for four generations, never spoke of this natural setting which belonged to his world long before I came along.

I had to leave the Mauricie and wait 40 years before I could fully appreciate one of autumn's stories. (Perhaps being away for 40 years brings about more vivid sensations of place.) The white corn swaying in the wind beneath a sky weighed down by dark grey clouds fills me with a sense of terror at once gentle and daunting. As a child I had never seen a spectacle as beautiful. I had never stepped into a landscape where the horizon looked like a folded eiderdown over the pasture and field, and under the quilt there was me. The trees in the forest had not yet lost their leaves. One shadow after the other began to move.

The Mauricie used to be fertile land. However, I should have abandoned it earlier, should not have witnessed the spectacle whose permanency would later escape my eyes, and my eyes themselves should have become weaker in order to better appreciate the vision granted to me. I had excellent eyesight at the time. Yet it seems to me that I noticed neither the overlapping of tamarack and birch trees on the plain, nor the beech trees in La Gabelle tightly grouped like men and women. Since my father passed away, I have learnt to "look" both for him and for myself. His silence nourishes the language I speak, his silence is the language I speak.

I now live in Quebec City. At times, when I stand on the road I live on I feel that I am walking, am in the city of Quebec. All this may sound redundant, the most obvious of truisms. But I call it my present tense. Time seems to have stopped. I know where to find the tame, urbanized tamarack, and I am glad I can. The present tense did not really exist for me. I have learnt to feel its rim. Proof is a pittance. I turn my eyes up and read the direction post with the name of the street I believe I am on, or feel I am on, or I am actually on, and for a couple of seconds I am the child I was when we used to visit Quebec City. Yet I don't lose sight of the fact that I am an adult wandering through a city that is a hearth for my heart: trees above my head, cars like waves on the make-believe fields of Chemin Sainte-Foy. The road is a few metres away from the house where I have become a father myself, and am speechless as I face the essential things of life. Perhaps such is the lesson we all must learn, with and without the help of our fathers, or with anybody else for that matter.

Such are the feelings within me at this moment, when I visit this city. There is a melody playing in this city that I have yet to grasp. Trees here never become red and yellow in the same way. An event is less intense than any drama. I recall the anxiety I felt back then, on a street, on a bike, or when I used to walk in the sunbright light of summer trapped in that small suburban town in the Mauricie, where no tree could protect me. I remember houses being built in the neighbourhood. How scary it all was. Our house was as well. All new. Cracking in winter like bones. The forest a few metres away, black before the turning red in autumn. The cornfield swaying like a pack of men in the wind.

I now live in an old house. I go for walks on the sunbright streets of my childhood and allow a dizzy spell rise silently within. I am not built to be new.

Translated, from the French, by Antonio D'Alfonso.

WINDOWS AND BEYOND

Paul Bélanger

Elemental time.

from WINDOWS AND BEYOND

The weather report you never listen to
except distantly and disenchantedly
when slouched in the melancholy of a sofa

the objects that face you quell their names
the cards from the world tip over
and the TV anchor's voice gets lost in the storm

you are frightened to admit it
but the woman's voice leaves you indifferent
nor does it disturb the paths within tangled
to the succession of the seasons

trees shed their leaves
the leaves turn trees green again
flowers scatter their dreams

among the clouds life begins anew
and stops like a sign
insignias of your absence

———

Evening fires in windows
statues lying in the garret
watch over the nervous city

to live in a voice dead
language forgotten language
to be reborn forgotten
by all words

I feel silence rising
dropping like dew
opening up to the murmuring dying

all I want is to watch
flowers and rivers

watching over the river watching

———

What climate
dog climate wolf climate
climate flood over plain

noontime darkness

what climate
in high season

into the heart of daybreak
a man trudges in
winter assaults him
and whips him with its ungraspable
anxiety

what climate
on the outrageous courage of the day

bodies agonizing rid of
their horizon bodies blessed
by feelings that cannibalize

———

Here is a man without a land
without a name without a country
he awakens like a tree
when his day is done

he crosses the river
and walks into the land shouting itself hoarse

absent and overwhelmed by voices
of lives lived against the grain he considers
the leaves falling onto the humus
in which his feet sink

the lone man looks towards the never-ending light
weakened in the sky turning red and

contemplates silence
with the patience of the wind

from RESPITE

1

resting day the river's without a wave
where I've come to find respite and feel
the pulse of time beneath my skin
                        one minute   one life

to fill up with forgetfulness
objects that return full circle – dust
kicked by the feet of greatness

listening to song deep in the promised space
of rifts where I carve out the first shapes
of time in the immeasurable bark

distant confession of words
chronicle of foretold absence
pleasure without end of strolling
in the steps of the first day

I'm no good at describing the headland
out there beyond the window water muddles
the moon as if it were a white eyeball dropping
into the river

63

one hour alone
I'll understand men once I
cross the threshold of this passageway again
demanding from ideas to impose
the single truth of this interpretative moment
when you the reader invent for me a word
born of fire and lightning
Ariadne's thread unwinding revealing
the day so to speak for the last thirty years
of which I moreover had no idea
once I discovered Rimbaud the Prince
a new life began to run through me from where
a number of poems remain yet this idea
I won't pursue so overtaken I am
by the disorder in my thoughts
without the final hour ever being near
stubbornly opening a parallel way
to the world and its moments
abstract flowers that were nothing but
silence in my memory
inexplicable and vertical instant
obsessive calling of voices
always with the word – and if none is found there
– I dig deep in the troubled waters of histories
nonstop and without respite in blood rising
to the surface of skin a bottomless wound
exaggeration is small if not mortal

I sharpen my knives and stab like a mongrel
in the joy of thoughts dismissing
pictures of newspapers even if
beyond the tragedy you return drunk with anxiety
who can find the belated name of the river
rising to history and each word
describing a labyrinth a story
of solitude whenever a single man returns
from his metamorphoses
in every second spreading him out
carrying him away making him larger
in the mosaic of memory
whenever a single man returns
as I was saying as though from a second existence
pointing on and on to intuition
as soon as you begin to walk into your tour
and display your biography
when in fact all you wanted to do was
to go out for some air on the bay's shoreline
of Rivière-Ouelle another day strolling
alone the endless expanse
facing the orient beyond the broken hills
like a skyline in my interior space
an ancient territory if I may call it that
the embraced space of the hour I tried
to retain in vain when I lose myself
— he who does not see life in the hour
vanishing what does he learn about himself
if he misses the rifts of the instant — time
to lie one letter beside another my being
beside myself rooting myself to earth
from the first echoes of life
from the past — visit the cathedral of
Notre-Dame du monde and find
a pillar that will listen to your confession —
all this useless time spent living
is not for nothing
words will climb over to the arches

where the Lord and his open-armed angels wait
like a page saturated by light bringing me back
to my wandering brothers who follow the genius of language
reinventing itself on the compromise
of dream's sheet of paper

all day has pushed its shadow
against my back the everyday oracle
encourages me to plunge into this moment
all ends

Author's Note: The poems included in Fenêtres et ailleurs *(Windows and Beyond) grew out of a need to capture the experience of landscape and painting as subject. At the time I was deep into Fernando Pessoa's poetry. Most of my books can be viewed as supplements to other books. Years later, I would publish* Le passeur du palais des ombres: Cahier de Fernando Pessoa à Montréal *(The Navigator of the Palace of Shadows: Fernando Pessoa's Montreal Notebook). As for the poems in* Répit *(Respite), they present themselves as echoes rising from the landscape around Rivière-Ouelle, on the south shore of the lower Saint Lawrence River.* Répit *was begun after I had completed a previous collection of poems, and so was meant to be a period of relaxation, and distancing. Hence its subtitle:* Journal of a Poem. *This work represents a space where poem meets voice.*

Translated, from the French, by Antonio D'Alfonso.

NOTES ON THE AUTHORS AND TRANSLATOR

Antonio D'Alfonso and Gilles Pellerin

When we speak of Québec, the image that immediately pops into mind is what Europeans might call "a landscape of plains". Québec is vast – it is not a country, this is true – and for many years people used to call it the *"pays d'en haut"* (the Upper Country) – an image that was coined by Claude Henri-Grignon, whose novel, *Un homme et son péché* (*A Man and His Sin*, 1933), was adapted for radio, film, television, theatre and comics.

Such things, however, do not concern much the contemporary Québécois writer, who often deplores the lack of acknowledgement for the not-so-young modernist school of French-language literature from Québec, so reflective of its society. Yet the one product from Québec which many citizens of Belfast would probably know of is Bombardier Aerospace, the major aeronautic firm. When leaving Québec for Belfast, when moving from one northern reality to another, one uses wings – and not the horse-pulled sleigh.

In the field of Québécois literature, there is a division on the east/west axis. By publishing both Paul Bélanger (western pole: Montréal) and Gilles Pellerin (eastern pole: Québec City), *Irish Pages* is offering a sample of the kind of work the two most important French-language literary and cultural centres this land of snow have to offer.

Born in Lévis, across the river from Québec City, the capital of the province of Québec, Paul Bélanger (b. 1953) was a published poet before becoming the publisher and editor-in-chief at Éditions du Noroît, widely considered the centre of French-language poetry, which celebrated its fortieth year of existence last year. The press's motto, "Le Noroît souffle où il veut" ("The north-easterly wind blows where it wishes"), exemplifies its mission, being the literary home of the largest spectrum of Québécois aesthetic traditions – and especially proud to be publisher of Québec's most important French-language poet, Jacques Brault.

With Éditions du Noroît, Paul Bélanger himself has published four of his own poetry books, one of which, *Origines des méridiens* (*Origin of the Meridian*, translated by Judith Cowan, and published by Signal Editions, 2010), was a finalist for a number of important awards, such as the Estuaire des Terrasses Saint-Sulpice Award, the Alain-Grandbois de l'Académie des Lettres du Québec Award, and the Governor General's Award. Another book, *Répit* (*Respite*), received the Alain-Grandbois de l'Académie des Lettres du Québec Award. In 2006, a selected poems, translated by Antonio D'Alfonso, appeared as *The World Forgotten* (Guernica Editions).

Gilles Pellerin (b. 1954) began his career as short-story writer at the same time as Paul Bélanger began his as a poet. In 1982, Pellerin published his first book, *Les sporadiques aventures de Guillaume Untel* (*The Sporadic Adventures of William Untel*, Asticou). Four years later, he became one of the founders of Instant Même, a press that specializes in publishing short fiction, its catalogue now listing 148 collections of short stories. Pellerin's own books are all short-story collections as well, though recently he has written extensively essays on questions of culture and literature, in *Récit d'une passion* (*Narrative of a Passion*, 1997) and *Nous aurions un petit genre* (*A Small Genre*, 1997), that reveal a fine thinker. His latest publications, all from Instant Même, are *ï* (*i tréma*, 2004), *Vingt-cinq ans de nouvelles* (*Twenty-five Years of Short Stories*, co-edited with Philippe Mottet), and *i²* (*i carré*, 2012), from which the preceding short fictions are taken – which are here translated into English for the first time.

A novelist, film-maker and editor, Antonio D'Alfonso (b. 1953) is the author of over 30 books. He founded Guernica Editions in 1978, where he published over 900 authors and 475 books. Since selling Guernica in 2010, he now works primarily as a literary translator and teaches creative writing, script-writing, film studies, and Italian at various universities. His novel *Un vendredi du mois d'août* (*One Friday in August*) won the Trillium Award in 2005. His feature film *Bruco* won Best Director Award and Best Foreign Film Award at the New York International Independent Film Festival in 2010. He has recently completed his next feature film, *Antigone* (an adaptation of Sophocles' play). He has a BA from Concordia University, a MSc from Université de Montréal, and a PhD from University of Toronto (all in film studies). He has translated some of the finest poets from Québec.

POEM

Patrick Deeley

NATURAL HISTORY

The last act of the huge pike – to swallow almost whole
a smaller rival. Which, before it dies, digs its way
half-through the gills of its attacker. Both specimens

float now in a formaldehyde jar, conflicted in one hunger
and one space for us to abhor, or find the nerve
to admire. Or there's a spaghetti ball of thread worms

extricated from the gizzard of another creature,
inducing a shudder. Or a wasp that makes a living larder
of the tarantula, so its own larva may survive.

On and on the dreadful devices, the live-or-die scenarios,
until we wonder if all's a case of cannibal existence
precluding redemption, and are shaken – as Darwin was –

out of the consoling notion of God as benign apotheosis
to which we aspire. Throw warfare into the hat,
throw barbarities we wage against earth and each other,

still somehow our morose hearts hold there exists a heaven
beyond the sway of instinct and natural wildness,
beyond the special sorrow saved for us, the aspirant angels.

Patrick Deeley was born in Loughrea, Co Galway in 1953. He is the author of one novel,
The Lost Orchard *(The O'Brien Press, 2001), and six collections of poems, most recently*
The Bones of Creation *(The Dedalus Press, 2010). He recently retired as a primary-school
principal, and lives in Dublin.*

THE FIFTH ELEMENT

Joseph Horgan

The wolf and the woodkerne.

Now it seemed logical to plunge into what Edward Thomas called the "fifth element": the element of wood.
(Roger Deakin, *Wildwood: A Journey through Trees*, 2007)

With the swallows gone there is suddenly a day when the wind whips through trees that are nearly bare. For some reason, some over-imaginative, Gothic reason, this brings the ravens to mind. They are the birds of storm and autumn, birds of solid darkness, birds of grim mythology. They are also, less anthropomorphically, a resident species, a big, dense bird that never leaves us. Something about that, with summer swallows departed, with leaves tumbling from trees, lends them a reassuring appeal. Simply, now that summer has left, the ravens can be relied upon because the ravens stay. Their presence is a fidelity that does not have to be marked by return.

One of the Irish names for Ireland was Inis na bhFiodhbhadh, the island of woods, a country that was heavily forested from coast to coast. I think of this as I set out to see the ravens. To reach their cliffside site I must pass through a small village and then a small patch of woodland. The raven site is not far from the closely cultivated fields surrounding the farmhouse I leave from, in the vicinity of the next parish but being, again, so much closer to the sea, a very different habitat. The small, coastal village curves around the shape of the bay, embracing the natural contour of the coast. The obligatory new housing estates sit at either end. The village and the estates are like two unconnected areas, two places far away from each other. Along the village there is a narrow line of sandy beach running beside the older settlement and just off this a path leading up to the woodlands. Beyond this I hope to find the very ravens that might possibly have lived there for a thousand years.

In autumn sunshine the sea to my left is deceptively calm. Past a few bungalows that look out across the water, I take the grass path to the woods and see the tall, heavy greenness of the trees ahead. This is old, mixed-deciduous woodland and there are trees at odd angles, trees lying where they have fallen. It ascends away from the coast and has a lively irregularity about it, the irregularity so many wooded plantations lack. The seasons course through this wood:

> In spring, the forest floor is carpeted in bluebells, which climb the slope to the right in a haze of purple. White ransoms, smelling of garlic, and delicate wood anemones, which close in the evening, are other flowers of the woods. There are a variety of mushrooms in autumn, including blewits, parasols and russula, and beechmast and hazel nuts ... Long eared owls nest in a tree hollow (Damien Enright, *Walks of Courtmacsherry Bay and The Seven Heads*, 1998).

I have seen this wood flooded with bluebells in spring, seen bees flocking around the honeysuckle, seen it sway in a coming Atlantic storm. Even now there is something about the woods, in the windblown lull between one season and the next, before winter proper bites in. Even now this small forest carries something intrinsically particular, something that reaches out. "To enter a wood is to pass into a different world in which we ourselves are transformed", wrote Roger Deakin. So, for a moment I stand still. I look up and across at the thin canopy above me. I see the sky through gaps in the green. I listen to the wood. There is a different presence here. This is a different place. This space completely belongs to the trees. The wind passing through it, the ocean beside it, the birds moving in it, the water that makes its way past it, all of these things do so through the element of the wood itself. The forest is the first thing. I am beneath the height of the trees, the beech and the thin, elegant birch, the occasional oak. Two bare paths testify to man's presence through here but this is not a managed place. A discarded can of beer and the occasional flutter of litter can sometimes be found here but they signify, where these trees are concerned, man's disregard, more his absence than his intent. There is thick undergrowth on the forest floor and enough loose wildness to suggest man's interference here is at a minimum. Beneath the trees, nearly falling off the coast on one side, the nearby ocean is forgotten. The glimpse of blue sea from time to time is reduced to a simple backdrop. It is the trees that hold sway here. Their soft, sibilant noise. Their grandness. Their completeness. Something other is here. Something the surrounding land, where trees are confined to hedgerows or the occasional small stand, does not possess. There is something fundamental here. Jean Giono's wonderful parable, *The Man Who Planted Trees*, comes to mind – the shepherd covering acres of war-torn land with the promise of trees because it "purifies and renews the earth about us, because it comforts us, and because it reconciles us to death". Something rudimentary, something elemental and indispensable is to be found beneath these tall specimens of the silent world. What can be touched here is simplicity, simplicity as an unadorned virtue: "The simplicity of song but more often of silence, and always of life" (André Comte-Sponville, *A Short Treatise on the Great Virtues*, 2003).

And simply standing beneath the trees seems to be enough to realize this: that this can be found here beneath these trees, in this small patch of woodland, in a corner of south-west Ireland that is only steps away from the ocean.

What is really wondrous though, what is truly rich here, is the realization of how diminished this all is. This small expanse of wood, carrying all that it does within it, is a mere flicker of what was once the dominant feature of this island. Ireland now has, whatever the impression those standing armies of conifers blocking the hillsides might give, one of the least amounts of tree cover in Europe. The island of woods is long gone. The forests of Ireland are now lost ones. So it is hardly surprising, even standing beneath the cover of this headland wood, that Frank Mitchell's words should ring so evocatively true and that it really is impossible for us to "picture the majesty and silence of those primeval woods, that stretched from Ireland far across northern Europe" (Frank Mitchell and Michael Ryan, *Reading the Irish Landscape*, 1997). All of that is gone from us. In that sense the landscape carries with it a sense of loss and this is intensified in the realization that, while what we call primeval or ancient woodland is something consigned to the vast stretches of the past, a forested Ireland is not. Even when man had begun to make extensive alterations to the aboriginal environment around him, even as the land began to be shaped by man's actions and original forest was cleared for fields and flocks, Ireland's tree-covered past survived well into documented, historical times:

> The extent and regenerative properties of the native forests were so great and powerful that, in spite of inroads of this and more intense kinds over the following thousand years, the greater part of the country even as late as the twelfth century was still clothed in trees (John Wilson Foster, *Nature in Ireland: A Scientific and Cultural History*, 1998).

Even writing of the Ireland of as late as 1600, the historian Roy Foster is able to state:

> Irish woods were famous: varied, dense and impenetrable to the unfamiliar. Willow, birch, hazel, pine, alder, oak, elm and ash were predominant, though the concentration varied: yew woods in Cork, oak in the southeast (Foster, *Modern Ireland, 1600–1972*, 1989).

The picture is truly that of a vanished environment, a heritage of forest, lost.

The destruction, when it came, came fairly rapidly and came not haphazardly but coherently. Irish woodland was felled for a variety of considered reasons, economic, cultural and military. Irish trees had been felled over the years as man's activities extended into forested areas but the final removal of the old tree-covered Ireland came about deliberately and intentionally:

> The systematic devastation of Irish woodlands followed rapidly on the unexpected defeat of the combined Irish and Spanish forces at Kinsale in 1601. As a result the substantially forested Ireland of 1600 had by 1711 become a treeless wilderness and a net importer of timber (John Wilson Foster, *Nature in Ireland: A Scientific and Cultural History*, 1998).

How much this must have changed the basic physical appearance of the country can only be imagined. If we have to struggle to picture Ireland's vast forests, we can barely glimpse what their destruction must have looked like. This was forestry clearance on a grand, commercial scale. With a government survey as late as 1623 reporting that Ireland abounded in good timber, at a time when timber was one of the prime goods of the world, the equivalent of today's oil, it is easy to see how ripe the environment of the newly colonized country was for wholesale exploitation. The removal of the forests would have affected every corner of the country, would have been felt by all of those living here:

> These half-felled woods were to be seen everywhere, even in the furthest places; there was, for instance, a great clearance made at

Coolmountain in West Cork (Daniel Corkery, *The Hidden Ireland: A Study of Gaelic Munster in the Eighteenth Century*, 1924).

That area is not too far from here, from the trees I now stand under, and is to this day a remote corner. If the clearances reached there it seems unlikely that many living here would have been untouched by such a fundamental alteration to their environment. Likewise, David Dickson writes that in the 1680s a great tract of land in this corner of Ireland was still "a large wooded country" and that in the "1650s there had been over 8,500 acres of woodland in the barony. However, by 1714 ... it was claimed with only slight exaggeration that not one acre of old timber remained" (David Dickson, *Old World Colony*, 2005). Even if there was no culture involving these forests, this is landscape alteration on a truly astonishing scale, especially in a non-industrial age. Another aspect of this first of the landscape traumas would have been, of course, not just the disappearance of the forests but of the myriad species of wildlife that existed within them – the deer and the goshawk, the wolf. All of these would have gone into a sudden decline. The physical environment of Ireland would have been altered beyond recognition. The whole natural world of the island would have been drastically different within the living memory of society. When the trees went, a whole biological existence, a whole ecological framework, went with them.

What also went with them, of course, was a way of being in Ireland, a cultural existence that was tied in with the natural world of the island in a way that is, once more, hard for a modern sensibility to grasp. The felling of the forests was not just a material clearance, it was a cultural one too. There was more than physical lumber taken from the land. For a people living on that land, in every sense of the word, their existence was such that it is not hard to believe that "they would have held the trees, mountains and other parts of the landscape in reverence" (David Hickie, *Native Trees and Forests of Ireland*, 2002). They existed within the framework of their immediate environment. The way they behaved and thought existed within the context of that environment. When "everywhere the giant woods were being cut down", this way of thinking was being cut adrift too. The physical landscape was being altered and the entire mind of a society that went with that was being utterly changed as well. Declan Kiberd writes that years later the remnants of that society still remembered this and that even well into the 1700s one could still have heard the "field labourers sing the great

Gaelic lament for fallen forests, Cill Cais" (Declan Kiberd, *Irish Classics*, 2000).

Cad a dhéanfaimid feasta gan adhmad?
Tá deireadh na gcoillte ar lár.
Now what will we do for timber,
with the last of the woods laid low?
(Seán Ó Tuama and Thomas Kinsella, *An Duanaire 1600–1900: Poems of the Dispossessed*, 1981)

The song mourns a way of life as much as it mourns the forest. The land, as those living on it would have realized, was being cleared not only in a material sense but metaphorically too.

That other way in which the woods were cleared is also a symbol of the way in which the Irish thought about the forests, for as their world changed around them in the early 1600s, the woodlands became their refuge; the trees became "gathering places of opposition" (John Wilson Foster) for what was, in effect, a defeated culture. The disappearing remnants of a collapsing society sought out the disappearing remnants of a collapsing environment. The new society that was arriving was well aware of this. It became such that to the new settlers on the new Irish landscape the woodlands and the Irish were inseparable. Irish soldiers, reduced to seeking out the forests as their last refuge, became known as "woodkernes". In the same regard they became synonymous with that other symbol of the forests, the wolf. In the imagination of the Ireland that was replacing them they became intertwined, the woodkerne and the wolf. Elizabeth I duly ordered that, apart from the economic aspects of felling, the woods be cleared to deprive the Irish and the wolf of this very shelter. The days of both the forested Ireland and the wolf were now numbered, the name of the Ireland that went with it too. The woodkerne and the wolf would soon be gone. The war waged on Irish soil became as much a war against the trees, against the Irish environment, as it was against anything else. The inhabitants of the island and the environment became as one.

It is little wonder that a society living on a heavily wooded island had developed a sensibility closely entwined with that natural context. It is little wonder that they had a folklore and set of beliefs around that natural context. It is little wonder that they sought it out as their last refuge. What is a wonder, though, is that within a short passage of time all the ideas of

Ireland, of natural Ireland, of authentic Ireland, would be those of a country without trees. The forests were no longer a part of the daily environment; they were no longer even the places of despairing refuge. In the light of all that went before, in the light of Ireland as the island of woods, of the woods as the last resting place of a defeated Irish culture, it is startling to realize that within two hundred years ideas of Irishness had changed so much, in a biological context at least, that trees were now seen as foreign. There was a general hostility to woodlands and "mutilation and cutting of trees became a common form of protest" (John Wilson Foster). The lost forests had gone from being an intrinsic part of the culture of the island and from being synonymous with the Irish themselves to being thought of as belonging to an imposed ascendancy class. The poet Austin Clarke put it very simply and clearly in his poem "The Planter's Daughter": "For the house of the planter / Is known by the trees." In a remarkable twist of biological history, woodland had now become synonymous with the newly arrived settlers, who had begun planting once they had finished clearing. With forests decimated, the psychology of the island had turned fully around. The Irish were no longer lamenting fallen trees; they were "mutilating" standing ones. So it was that the archetypal image of the Irish landscape became the austere beauty of a green, treeless one. So it was that the splendour of an expansive, unbroken sweeping Connemara became the standard example of what Ireland truly looked like. So it was that those who sought a cultural revival of Ireland in the early 1900s turned to that western seaboard as the genuine and authentic embodiment of what constituted Irishness. It was as if the destruction of the great forests had not only erased them from the material, physical landscape but also from the nurturing recesses of the Irish mind.

The distraction in these woods that I stand in is that they carry the echoes of all that history. These woods are old but they are planted. They are probably part of the old Earl of Shannon estate, part in themselves of the traumatic history of forests on this small island. In the earlier days of forest clearance the Boyles, the Earl of Shannon family, were eagerly involved in the profitable timber industry. At a time in the early decades of the 1600s when Cork was exporting "vast quantities of hardwood barrel staves", the family recorded "private transactions involving some four million staves" (David Dickson). They were clearing away the forests of Ireland, clearing the forest from this corner of the island. Yet, following the path of other planter families, this and other woods were planted by a Boyle descendant at a time when, even before the 1600s had elapsed, the very same sections of society that had removed the great forests were expending huge amounts of capital on horticulture, landscaping and trees. Natural-style parks soon came into vogue with a "new appreciation that 'natural' features, such as woods, streams and hills, were beautiful in themselves and indeed good for the soul" (John Wilson Foster). What had been taken away was now thought of as most advantageous to put back in. Now that nature had been tamed it was to be regulated and given discipline and order. The landscape, in this way of viewing it, is always a blank canvas, awaiting realization. There is, of course, the old colonial element here too, of something, in this case the land, having no intrinsic value until "discovered" – even if that discovery involved denuding and then replenishing with the very same thing that was first taken away.

This woodland is a part of all that. Of all that destruction. Of the change of forest from intrinsically Irish to intrinsically foreign. This woodland is a palimpsest: layer upon layer of the Irish past beneath the trees. Once settlers like the Earl of Shannon began their replanting enterprises, of which this wood is almost certainly originally a part, the trees took on a different symbolic existence on the island. They were not now characteristic of the wooded island itself but characteristic of the demesne. Outside the demesne, Ireland was usually recorded in the same way – "a dreary waste where, there is scarcely a twig sufficient to form a resting place to the birds fatigued with their flight" (John Wilson Foster). Trees became things that were confined to a certain place, a certain physical and cultural place. They were now seen, by their planters at least, as signs of improvement and superior culture. Then, in a circular sense early Irish artists might have recognized, the demesne trees too came up against man's political, cultural and economic design. Once Ireland's Free State came into being, the demise of the demesne was not far behind, as the old ascendancy land became unsustainable for a declining economic and political class. The demesne estates were sold off and the woodlands met a now-familiar end. "By the 1920s Ireland's woodland had shrunk, from 340,000 acres in 1880, to about 130,000 acres" (John Wilson Foster). Much of that was to do with the breakup of those old estates. Not far from here, further back up the coast, in the grounds of a still-standing, Gothic old demesne, there is a walk to be taken amongst acres of wooded land. It is mainly conifer plantation now. Mary Carbery, the wife of Lord Carbery, kept a reflective, moving and sometimes beautiful diary of her time living there between 1898 and 1901. She writes deeply of the woods there, of their variety and their "greening beech trees" and "indescribable loveliness" (Jeremy

Sandford, *Mary Carbery's West Cork Journal 1898–1901*, 1998). Those woods are gone now, replaced by a monotone plantation. Wooded Ireland had reached another stage.

But these woods themselves, although so much a part of that, are also beyond all that. They occupy another space that stands apart from that of the emblematic, beyond that of lost worlds or considerations of Ireland's material legacy. While it is hard to ignore the steady procession there has been through the space and time of our wooded landscapes, something that has created the places of today, none of that, for this moment, holds sway. For this moment, as I stand beneath these trees, this space is just itself and for this time it is just the woods and me. It is the life of the wood that I can see and hear and feel. Mary Carbery, so moved by her own woodlands, wrote from her neo-medieval home on that headland of the remote west-Cork coast at the turn of the twentieth century that "isolation means a deeper love and sense not of possession, but of being a part of something essential" (Jeremy Sandford). I recall her words now as I stand beneath the trees, as I listen, as I walk through them. Something in the woods is essential, something calls our steps on. For we have always been amongst trees. They are amongst the largest, longest-lived things on our planet. Through most of human life our fortune has gone hand in hand with theirs. The noise they now create, as the wind rises, is one that most of our ancestors would have had as the primary noise of their lives. There is the unavoidable, unscientific sense that they have some kind of sensibility, some sort of sentience. An awareness. There is a comfort in being here, in standing beneath them, in walking through them. Something that comes from them, from their physical presence. The trees bring us back. They root us. Though it is many lives since humans on this island lived amongst them to any great extent, there is still the unadorned sense, standing beneath them, of being at home.

Reliably, heavily, the ravens are there. It would be hard to miss them. These largest of the crows are an impressive size and they have an obvious sturdiness about them. As I come out on the path that runs beside the coast the solidity of the raven stands out amongst the flight and movement of other birds. Sitting high in the branches of a cliffside gorse, the single bird I come across makes no attempt to hide or disappear. Though it is said that they are a bird that has not, unlike other crows, adjusted well to civilization and are found instead in these wilder, uninhabited places, this is clearly not accompanied by any timidity. This bird seems almost arrogant, or at the least completely unperturbed by my presence, though there is the watchful awareness that is to be expected from any intelligent crow. I look out to sea for a while and when I turn back the bird is still sitting in full view, impassively. The raven, a long-established European species, now occupies only a portion of its former range but their reassuring presence here reflects their ancient status. "Around 2,000 BC ravens kept company with other Neolithic birds", their history states, "so it does not seem particularly far fetched to imagine this territory as being occupied by an unbroken tenancy of ravens" (Sylvia Bruce Wilmore, *Crows, Jays, Ravens*, 1977). They have been around us for a long time, long embedded in man's imagination. It is also true that individual birds have been recorded as enjoying a life span that exceeds that of most others. Though their lives in the wild are unpredictable, tamed ravens have lived for up to 50 years, with one individual purportedly living to an amazing 69 years of age. Though this is most unlikely, if not impossible in the wild, it is still an astonishing capability for a bird to possess. When I turn back again after watching the endless ocean, the bird is impassively sitting there. They are territorial, the guide book says, and "their mere physical presence is enough to stake a claim". Looking at the strong bird behind me, I do not find that hard to believe. As far as the bird is concerned, I get the impression that we are looking out to sea as equals. There is from time to time the occasional gust of strong wind coming in from the ocean, but the raven merely rides the rising of the branch the way a gull might sit astride a wave. Their plumage apparently has a purple or green sheen but I see nothing but unspoiled black. Recorded as nesting as early as January, there is an unrelenting ruggedness about the raven. On the coasts it frequents it is thought of as the master of the air and even with the hardiness that most species on the fringe here have it is not hard to see why that might be true. Like other corvids, the ravens mate and stay together for life. The bird I look at now will probably spend all of its life along this patch of coast. Somehow all of these factors – the antique status of the species, their possible longevity, their faithfulness to site and partner, their physical solidity – creates a reassuring presence. The English poet John Clare wrote of this very thing in his poem "The Raven's Nest":

> … where still they live
> Through changes winds and storms and are secure
> And like a landmark in the chronicles
> Of village memorys treasured up yet lives
> The hugh old oak that wears the raven's nest.

An enduring raven's nest becomes, in that sense, like a repository of our memory. Emblems of our mythology, they are birds that have always been around us and we around them. Even though they have retreated now to these wilder, untamed, less-bothered places, there is still a connection between us. The raven that sits now easily, almost playfully on the outcrop of gorse, this spot where Damien Enright fancied a raven family may have been for a millennium, offers a connection with a previous country, a continuum when so much is being discarded that, as I stand here buffeted by Atlantic winds, is like an anchor. When there is, as now, such a disjuncture between society and the natural landscape, it is something of a comfort that the raven, the master of the coast, is the master yet.

Making my way back along the path and coming up again to the beginning of the woodland I stand once more and look back. The sea stretches away from me. From where I stand on this windy, autumn day, I can see far off in the distance the furthest finger of land. It is now an exclusive golf club, but that headland is the Old Head of Kinsale and is the very same place where those Irish forces were defeated in 1601 and where the ultimate demise of the old Gaelic order can be said to have commenced. Soon enough, too, it marked the thorough and final clearance of the remaining Irish woodlands, a history the beautiful woods I am about to re-enter are so much a part of.

From the woods to the ravens and back again our memory is stored. There is cold now. The wind picks up and there is sea-spray in the air. I seek the shelter of the trees.

The above essay is a chapter in Joseph Horgan's forthcoming non-fiction volume, The Song at Your Backdoor *(The Collins Press).*

A poet, non-fiction writer and reviewer, Joseph Horgan was born in 1964 and raised in Birmingham, England, by Irish immigrant parents. He has lived in West Cork since 1999. He is the author of two poetry collections, most recently An Unscheduled Life *(Agenda Editions, 2012), and writes a weekly column for* The Irish Post *in Britain.*

POEMS & TRANSLATIONS

Chris Preddle

NEW HELEN

If you or I or Under-the-Sky came down
from Issues Road and Meal Hill
with our human anxiety like a hem undone,

if we came down to Holme
and Watery Lane and Rake Lane
and lifted the hood of selfhood like a helm,

how the external, matter earthen and carnal,
comes up against us. That city-state
of Holme and its habitations, cattle, fruit trees, cornland

and whatever else may be numerically stated,
are what is. Though we ourselves
name and number them under the sky, they are constituted

that in which we may find what avails us,
what also is. And even as we decline
down Meal Hill and Rake Lane, we meet there other selves,

Achilles in his helm, Heloise veiled, a sweet colleen
of the Clyde or Caryae or the County Down,
all the hooded and lost, and new Helen in Jacqueline.

AND CAME JACQUELINE

And came Jacqueline upriver from her coast
against the swim
of things, against the shallows and shoals that would assume
they were grounds for something. Swam like a Jacqueline Cousteau
in the schools
of fish and scholars, sophies
and Sufis and cod philosophers.
Emerged upriver at Holme in her mermaid scales
and her own sophrosyne,
her passionate mindfulness. Someone had there foreseen her.

And came to a snowland, the white of an eye
of Arthur felled
in his imperfections, his length all England. On a snowfield
Ever-Since or you or I
went about in anxiety. Our history
has failed;
we decline, we noble knyghtes tinfoiled,
to doo after the good and leve the evyl; our island-story
has no moral. Came
among the helmed uneasy Is on an icefield
fouled
like the field of Camlann. Came
hawthorn, white. Came as the other, she or he or Who-May-Be
who is whatever value there may be.

And came south, from the saltwater Battery Baths
of Greenock, to a green wood sun-
leafed in Aix. Cézanne
would paint her forever among the river bathers.

And came ashore at Cyprus. In the Dome Hotel
in a queensize bed or sea-bed
she listened to the sowff
and suffer
of the sea. To love and be loved is not so bad.
In the green McCartney dress I'm tall
as a cypress. And stood at the pier-glass and pinned
her yellow hair, with the sea-windows open.

And came uphill to the Abbey of Peace
in ruins, its medieval stone
stolen
like peace of mind. She was taken piece by piece.

DYLAN AND JACOB

Dylan and Jacob came, boys in an attic
leaf-level-living, mantic antic
Jacks-in-the-Green. Grown, in their court or hallmote
they judged, to a haulm,
the times they lived like leaves in. They saw from a garret
Europe, its once beginnings, and furthest Asia sea-girt.

They saw the Christian West subside
like Ys in the sea. It carried all to the seabed,
Logos and reason and Lyonesse. Whatever else we were,
we'd been in the wars. O boys of the airy elsewhere,
see what we made, what shapes, how absolute,
as the age unmade itself, an ether unstable.

SAPPHO 55

And after death you'll lie there, never be thought of again
and not be missed in future. You've not shared
the Muses' roses. Flown and in Hades too unknown
you'll meander up and down with the dim and dead.

SAPPHO 94

"And I honestly wish I was dead!"
She was crying at leaving me behind,

and time and again she said,
"What a terrible time we've had!
Oh Sappho, I hate to leave you so."

I answered her: "Go,
and be happy. Remember me,
you know how much we cared for you.

If you don't, I want to remind you
of the good times we used to have.

So many crowns of roses and violets,
circlets of crocuses
you crowned your hair with, next to me,

so many flowers you wove
in garlands and
garlanded your soft neck for me,

so many perfumes flower-drawn,
the scented oil
of queens, you wore like an ample ointment.

On soft beds you'd satisfy your passion.

There was never a holy place or shrine
from which we stayed away,
not a grove, a dance, a sound ..."

SAPPHO 96

In Sardis, often it's here she's thinking of.
She thought you like
some famous goddess and most of all loved your singing.

Now she stands out among Lydian women
as clear as the moon
when the sun's set, a rose-red-fingered moon

surpassing all stars; it extends
an equal light
on the salt sea and over flowering lands;

and a beautiful dew's come down, poured out,
and roses and delicate
chervil have flowered thickly, and melilot.

As she comes and goes she remembers you,
her gentle Atthis,
and for what you suffer heart's-longing eats her through.

SEA-NAME

And came Jacqueline south, as one in a myth
comes to an island of serviceable pines,
whose pins and needles
go sliddering down the path to the beach. No needless
goats or Pan
go down to her naked rock. The bay opens its mouth
to the quop and slop
of the sea at the foot of the great sea-slope.
And fifty nereids came ashore
and sang her a sea-name like their own.
By that and this she shall be known,
nereid sunning by the green sea-door.

Sappho: early Greek female poet, celebrated from antiquity until the present day, whose surviving corpus consists of about 200 poems and fragments.

Chris Preddle has retired from libraries to a windy shoulder of the Pennines in West Yorkshire. His second collection is Cattle Console Him *(Waywiser, 2010); his first was* Bonobos *(Biscuit, 2001). He is translating all of Sappho's poems and fragments.*